SUCCESS, MONEY & HAPPINESS DEMYSTIFIED

All rights reserved.

No part of this publication may be reproduced or transmitted in any form or by any means without permission from the publisher. The moral right of the author has been asserted. Every effort has been made to contact the copyright holders. Those copyright holders whom we have been unable to contact are requested to contact the publisher, so that omission can be remedied in the event of a reprint.

Copyright © Marc Pillay 2023

First edition published in January 2024
Paperback ISBN: 978-1-77933-779-5
Publisher: Marc Pillay – Demystifying Life
Email: lifedemystified.inc@gmail.com
Author page: https://www.amazon.com/author/marcpillay

Editing: Jennifer Cole
Cover: wim@wimrheeder.co.za
Book production: Liquid Type Publishing Services

Set in 10.5 point on 15 point, Caecilia

SUCCESS, MONEY & HAPPINESS
DEMYSTIFIED

MARC PILLAY

MARC PILLAY
DEMYSTIFYING LIFE

amazon
Amazon Author Page

https://www.amazon.com/author/marcpillay

https://www.facebook.com/
marcpillay.demystifyinglife/

@pillay_marc

ABOUT THE AUTHOR

Marc Pillay is married with two beautiful children – a daughter aged 7 and a son aged 5.

Marc is a life-analyst, aiming to demystify a host of life situations by questioning conventional wisdom and the status quo; by analysing common life scenarios and continuously aiming to unpack them in a way that provides practical, day-to-day value; by asking real questions applicable to real-life situations; and by giving real answers that every-day people can identify with and put into practice to improve their lives.

This is Marc's fourth published book, and third in his Demystified series. He has also had a number of business and legal articles published on various national and global platforms, including the biggest national newspaper in Zimbabwe and www.commonwealthlawyers.com.

Marc is a lawyer by profession, with 20 years' experience, cutting across private practice and the corporate sector.

CONTENTS

PREFACE
I was successful but miserable   9

PART I – INTRODUCTION
Chapter 1 – The Trap   13

PART II – HAPPINESS
Chapter 2 – Sunny Days   21
Chapter 3 – The Happiness Score   29
Chapter 4 – Make Yourself Happy   39
Chapter 5 – Happiness versus Pleasure   49
Chapter 6 – Nostalgia   57

PART III – PEOPLE
Chapter 7 – Needs and Desires   65
Chapter 8 – Who are you trying to impress?   73
Chapter 9 – Impress Yourself   81
Chapter 10 – The Different Shades of You   87

PART IV – MONEY
Foreword on Money   95
Chapter 11 – Money: Illusion and Obsession   99
Chapter 12 – More Money, More Problems   121
Chapter 13 – Would you quit your job?   129
Chapter 14 – The cost of Money   151
Chapter 15 – Peace of Mind   165

PART V – SUCCESS

Chapter 16 – Will the real success please stand up — 175
Chapter 17 – Path and Purpose — 185
Chapter 18 – Ikigai — 201

PART VI – CONCLUSION

Chapter 19 – Success and Happiness: Joined at the hip — 229
Chapter 20 – Bringing it all together — 235

APPENDIX A

The different shades of you — 251

APPENDIX B

How the law turned debtors into kings — 261

NOTES

267

PREFACE

I WAS SUCCESSFUL BUT MISERABLE

> "After high school came law school and then a career as a litigation lawyer. I was successful but miserable."

This could well be an excerpt from my early adult life story. Well ... sort of. My mother, my wife and my sister all took the initial assumption that I was speaking about myself when they read my first draft, and an educated guess tells me that most readers who know me on any personal level came to the same immediate conclusion. Coincidental as it may be this statement comes from a piece posted by Robin Sharma on one of his social media platforms. The post itself is several paragraphs long, but it was five words in particular that instantaneously leapt out at me as I read the post:

> "I was successful but miserable."

I immediately went through the dozens of comments beneath the post. Seemingly nobody had picked up this enormously conspicuous irregularity. And its absence of any mention in the comments section represented, somewhat, a microcosm of life and the way society has come to view and define "success". So many people – no, *too many people* – just don't see any anomaly; any contradiction; any inherent flaw; any oxymoronic properties in the statement "I was successful, but miserable." And what made this assertion even more bizarre was the fact that it had been made by one of *the* "success gurus" of our time.

But what's all the fuss about being successful but miserable? It's a statement that, on the face of things, probably describes millions of working adults globally, right? I have no doubt that many will, as they read this, be thinking "yup, that sounds a lot like me." Well, here's the thing. The whole notion of "success" must, surely, exclude the scope for misery. How is it even possible to label oneself "successful" when it is founded upon misery? Can success and misery coexist in the same person, or are they mutually exclusive? Isn't happiness a core component of success? Or shouldn't it be? And if so, how does this happiness exist and survive in an environment of misery?

This very simple, ostensibly accurate, and highly applicable statement set off a concatenation of questions in my mind, each one triggering another, like a long line of dominoes. Questions that I found myself compelled to thrash out and answer, not only for myself but for the millions of people who mindlessly accept that it is possible to be "successful but miserable". It is my assertion that such a state does not, and simply cannot, exist! And this book explains why.

PART I
INTRODUCTION

CHAPTER I

THE TRAP

Allow me to go back to Sharma's thought-provoking statement that forms the very foundation of this book. "I was successful but miserable." There will be several references to it as we go on, such is its importance. What many a person will have "read" in that statement is:

> "I was *financially* successful but miserable."

By adding just one extra word, the statement suddenly makes a whole lot more sense. The state of being *financially* successful but miserable is one that not only *can* exist but *does* exist on a very large scale. To certain sections of the global population, this state is their norm. Let's look at a 2019 survey by global analytics firm Gallup.[1] (I shall refer to this as "the Gallup Survey" in later chapters.) Without getting into the methodology of the analysis, it revealed that a whopping 85% of the estimated one billion full time employees globally "hate their job and especially their boss". Now it seems obvious that if you hate your job, which accounts for a third of the 24 hours we all have in a day, and half one's waking hours, then you are most certainly miserable!

Let's dig a bit deeper into what *should be* obvious but in reality is not. If you hate your job, and your boss, then why do you keep going back for more misery ... day after day, week after week, month after month? The broad answer is, quite simply, money. Every employee goes to work, first and foremost, for the pay cheque that is received every month. The *quid pro quo* for hour upon hour; day upon day of misery. Beyond this broad answer, however, lie two categories of employee – both motivated by money, but for different reasons.

- The first category comprises those who earn just about enough to cover their needs from pay cheque to pay cheque with little, if any, room for small comforts and embellishments from time to time to take the edge off the struggle and strain of day-to-day life. The motivation is survival. This category is commonly referred to as "low-income earners". For many in this category job opportunities are not particularly easy to come by, so they stay where they are, grin and bear the misery, and try to focus instead on the survival of themselves and their families. If other opportunities do arise, it is often a case of "better the devil you know". So, they stay where they are and the misery continues.
- The second category is made up of two sub-categories: those commonly known as middle- and high-income earners respectively. But

this distinction is largely irrelevant to the point being made. This broader group, unlike the first one, doesn't live from pay cheque to pay cheque. Actually, let me rephrase that: this group doesn't *need to* live from pay cheque to pay cheque. If they do that, it is down to financial irresponsibility and indiscipline; and, in many cases, trying to keep up with the Joneses rather than through necessity. The point is that people in this category can afford to meet their needs with varying levels of comfort, and then have something left over for whatever tickles their fancy. It could be saving for a rainy day, investing, upgrading one's car or house, or going on holiday. There are countless possibilities. This category earns enough to afford a lifestyle that paints a picture of "success" on some level. They are not just "getting by" but are "doing well". They, too, grin and bear the daily misery, but the focus is on the good money, and the "success" that comes with it. It is these people that are "successful but miserable". More accurately speaking, of course, they are *financially* successful ... but miserable.

It is the second category that best illustrates the trap. The trap that has been set by society over generations. Not only have certain people fallen into it and been fooled into thinking they are successful, but many around them have been deceived into the same assumption. How many times have you seen an expensive performance car drive past, and someone in your company (if not you, yourself) instinctively quips, "Wow! He must be successful."? And the other members of the group, equally instinctively, nod in approval. We all do this from time to time, some more frequently than others. And often, it is subconscious. The fact that so many people completely and routinely discard the need for the critical qualification – *financially* successful – is a clear indication of a certain mindset. An erroneous, yet default mindset that has developed among human beings. A mentality that if you are financially successful, you have attained this thing called "success"; that if you arrive at the destination that is financial success, then it is a natural consequence that all other important aspects of your life must also have followed the same path of success.

This, of course, is a fallacy. And it would be abundantly clear to anyone who just paused for a few minutes to consider that a person's financial standing – whether their own or someone else's – is not the be all and end all in life. But few people actually do this. Instead, we mindlessly associate money with success. We instinctively assume that because a person is financially successful (or merely appears to be financially successful) the other aspects of his life must be equally as good as his bank balance (or the bank balance he appears to have). And by extension we robotically take it as a given that all aspects of our own lives will magically improve in direct proportion to any increase in our income. When we get a promotion and a 20% salary increase, it must surely follow that our lives will be 20% better. And there it is – the trap! Or rather, the Trap, which will be referred to frequently throughout this book.

The effect of the Trap is to compel people to do whatever they can to earn more money (which often means subjecting themselves to more misery). Because the more money we have, the more we will be viewed as successful – both by ourselves and by those who meet us. Or even those who just catch a glimpse of us driving past in that expensive new car (which will probably take years and years to pay off, and is costing a small fortune in interest alone in the meantime, but hey ... who cares about that, right? Nobody even needs to know!). But the reality, to reiterate, is that money will not automatically improve all aspects of life. Not even close! In fact, in many cases it can lead to the opposite, something we look at in more detail in part IV.

We become trapped in the rat race. The bulk of our time and energy is focused on earning more money. But it never really ends. If anything it becomes a chronic disease which is, perhaps, the only logical way to explain the very existence of this species called the billionaire. These people must have fallen so deep into the Trap that they couldn't stop trying to earn more money, even though they already have enough to last 1000 lifetimes. Literally! The word "billionaire" has come to represent some sort of ultra-success. It has become a title and a status symbol, rather than merely an adjective. The person with a billion dollars, however, is not any different from the person with a fortune of 990 million dollars, save for one aspect – the latter falls short of the coveted title *billionaire*.

As we the commoners look from the outside through the lenses that the media provides and even forces upon us, it's not difficult to see that even for this exclusive club that makes up less than 0.0000004%[2] of the global population, life is not all a bed of roses. In recent years we've seen two of the world's most preeminent billionaires – Jeff Bezos and Bill Gates – getting divorced. We've seen another billionaire – Kanye West – getting divorced, losing sponsorship deals, and having an honorary doctorate rescinded among other things.

Several studies have been done over years and decades, and invariably they all conclude that divorce is in the top three most stressful live events for any person. Who wants that level of stress, regardless of how much money you have? Stress aside, I imagine it must be a pretty big blow to the ego, particularly a billionaire male ego, for a woman to tell you that she no longer wants to be your wife. Isn't the person with less money but a happy marriage and a contented personal life, in a sense, more successful than the one with ridiculous amounts of money but a broken marriage and the consequent strained relationships with their children?

If you don't take a bit of time to reflect on what your success really is (and we look at this in detail in Part V), you will inevitably fall into the Trap and spend your life primarily chasing *financial* success. And whether you come to the realisation or not, it *will* be at the expense of all the other good things in life. And you *will* fall deeper and deeper into the Trap. Don't allow yourself to!

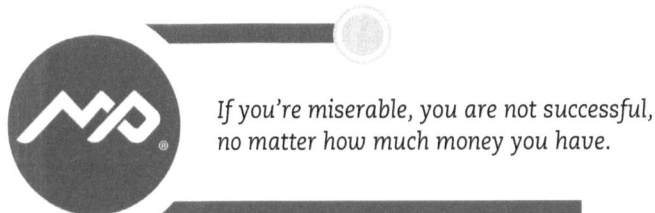

If you're miserable, you are not successful, no matter how much money you have.

PART II
HAPPINESS

CHAPTER 2

SUNNY DAYS

Have you ever asked yourself, like *really* asked yourself, "What makes me happy?" And if so, were you able to answer it with any level of accuracy?

The reality is that many of us never really stop to give this question any conscious and focused attention. Instead, we wander through life like robots that have been programmed only for financial success. Perhaps that *is* what we've become. With the underlying, largely subconscious, assumption that when we attain this thing called financial success we will automatically, and somewhat miraculously, be happy. As if happiness is the natural and inevitable consequence of financial success. And while we're on that pre-programmed journey to the place called financial success, we will get by on cheap thrills like a new pair of shoes (that we really don't need) on payday, and the odd beach holiday to take our minds off the 8-5 job that we don't really like. These are our small doses of "happiness" as we traverse this miserable path to financial success. And then the next, more miserable path towards greater financial success. Of course, we make sure to take lots of photos of those new shoes and that holiday (and whatever else), because we need to post them all over social media in a bid to convince all our "friends" that we are happy. Or is it to show them that we're successful? We're not really sure. Maybe its *ourselves* more than anyone that we're trying to convince? Perhaps we've become so dependent on those social media likes and comments as a means to fill the void of an unfulfilling life? Whatever the case, this assumption that happiness automatically follows financial success – this pre-programming by which so many of us mindlessly operate – is not only wide of the mark, but also quite ridiculous if you think about it rationally. By this reasoning that happiness follows financial success, happiness is effectively out of the reach of most of the world's population. This surely cannot be the reality of life. Surely!

A few years ago, I began a daily practice of making a mental list of the things that I was grateful for, and I would offer up a prayer of thanksgiving for those things. Let's call it my *Gratitude List*. There are certain things that find their way onto this list daily, chief among them being my children and their wellbeing. And there are others that are more specific to certain days. The ad-hoc guest stars on my list, like my flight arriving at its destination safely. There is no doubt that there are many things that don't make it onto the list but probably should. While I'm trying to be more consciously grateful for even the small things, I remain guilty of taking things for granted, which is what we too often do as human beings. Incidentally, this could well be one of the biggest reasons that the quest for happiness appears to be so elusive to humankind. This brings me to a particular conversation I had with my wife a couple of years ago, which I must recount before getting back to my gratitude list.

I took a deep breath, rolled my eyes, and braced myself for the latest episode in what had become a long running series of uncomfortable discussions that my wife would resuscitate every few months. In a nutshell, she wanted to leave Zimbabwe, where we lived. I did not. That had been the state of affairs for years. This would prove to be the final episode in this series of difficult discussions. While there were still many positives to life in Zimbabwe, the negative aspects had begun to outweigh the positives. On this occasion, at last, I conceded that things were not going to improve. The light at the end of the tunnel – the promise of improvement – which had always formed one of the key components in my previous arguments, and which had always resulted in a stay of execution, was now patently extinguished. Perhaps it had gone out long before and I just hadn't noticed or, more likely, I refused to notice, until then. Sadly (for me at least), it was time to begin planning a new life away from my beloved Zimbabwe.

The obvious next question was "Where to?" My wife's first choice was the UK and she had various good reasons. But I immediately vetoed that destination. And my reasons? Well, there was only one. The weather! All my life I had enjoyed – what I now recognise as the privilege it was – the perfect Zimbabwean climate, and I was not prepared to surrender to the miserable UK weather. It was the first time I had consciously thought about something seemingly as simple as the weather, and I quickly came to realise its huge influence on my state of mind and, in essence, its grave importance in my day-to-day life. I remember my words vividly, and that was long before I had any ideas of writing a book about happiness.

> "No matter how much more money we may end up earning, we can never buy the weather."

In short, sunny days make me happy. For me, it's not enough to be able to afford holidays to sunny destinations for a few weeks every year. Not even close! Something as simple as sunny days is an integral component of my day-to-day and overall happiness, and that will trump financial success every time.

We've since settled in the Kingdom of Bahrain. The summer months are brutal … if you choose to (or must) brave the outdoors or remain in the country at all over those summer months. But if you're as fortunate as I am, you have the privilege and pleasure of sitting in an air-conditioned office (in my case a work-from-home office) with spectacular views of clear skies and the turquoise and azure patches of the Persian Gulf dancing under the disco ball that is the brilliant Arabian sun. I'm no longer in my beloved Zimbabwe, but I've got my sunny days. And that makes me happy.

Since that conversation with my wife, "sunny days" has made it onto my daily gratitude list. My typical gratitude list looks like this:

1. That I have happy and healthy children
2. That my children love me unconditionally
3. That I am in good health
4. That I have a healthy marriage
5. That I have good relationships with my immediate family members
6. That my immediate family members are in good health
7. That the sun is shining outside
8. That I am financially okay

Everyone should have a gratitude list, which I'll explain further in a moment. Just as every person will have a different idea of what happiness means to them, each person's gratitude list will, naturally, be different. And here we begin to see a nexus emerging, an inherent relationship between gratitude and happiness. You see, in formulating a gratitude list, there is a certain thought process that must necessarily kick in. It is a thought process that almost forces you into a state of happiness! It is invaluable, and it looks something like this:

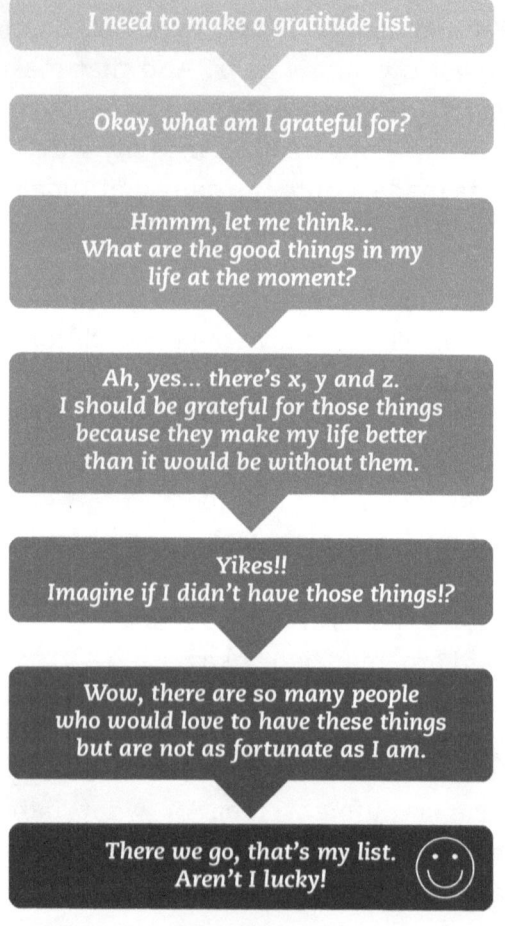

Fig 2.1 – Creating a gratitude list.

*It is perhaps worth specifically mentioning that reference to "things" is very broad. It does not refer exclusively to material things!

My own gratitude list clearly demonstrates the huge subjective element of this concept of happiness. My children will always be at the top of my list. But there are billions of people out there who don't have children. There are also billions who don't get 300 sunny days a year. Those people will be, and certainly should be, thankful for very different things. Very different things that, nonetheless, make them as happy as my children and sunny days make me. To reiterate, when you make a gratitude list you force yourself to become consciously aware of, and thankful for, certain things that make you happy and, equally importantly, of the fact that you would be significantly less happy without them. There is an unavoidable, and wholly positive, shift in mindset.

Start by deciphering what it is that makes you happy. What really makes you happy. You owe it to yourself!

CHAPTER 3

THE HAPPINESS SCORE

The concept of happiness is a strange one. On the one hand, as I touched on in the previous chapter, it is highly subjective. A moving target if you will. One that shifts each time it is looked at through a different set of eyes. Different people, quite simply, have different ideas on the meaning of happiness. Perhaps more pertinently, the meaning of happiness *to them*. And so they should. There are thousands, probably millions if you look long enough, of different definitions of happiness that can be found at the touch of a button. They are no more than opinions. Opinions based largely on the personal experiences, preferences and circumstances of each person who has attempted to define the concept. On the other hand, however, and despite the obvious subjective element, I am convinced that there must be a universally acceptable understanding of happiness.

We live in an age where there is a constant compulsion to measure. To measure anything and everything. This is not necessarily a bad thing if you subscribe, as I do, to two schools of thought: "If it exists it can be measured" (E. L. Thorndike) and "If you don't measure it, you can't manage it" (Professor Robert Kaplan). Problems only arise where there is what I call a *misguided* compulsion to measure; where we measure anything we can. Often completely pointless metrics, but metrics nonetheless, purely for the sake of measuring and being able to then say that we did, in fact, measure. And then we tick a box and move on, just as oblivious as we were before. It is a pointless exercise if we don't consider how that measurement tells us what we need to know, or whether it does at all. My first book, *Life Demystified*, goes into much more detail in a chapter entitled *The Misguided Compulsion to Measure*.[3]

In the context of happiness the point is quite simply that it, too, should not only be *capable* of being measured, but should *actually be* measured. Such a measure would be far more important and useful than any of the broad, subjective definitions thrown out, many of which carry little meaning in the absence of some contextual explanation from the originator. The major underlying constraint that we face in trying to assign any meaningful measure to happiness is, you guessed it, the Trap! It represents the easy, but erroneous, way out. To put it simply, money is a measure. An easy measure. Unfortunately, it is not a measure of success (to be distinguished from *financial* success), and it is most certainly not a measure of happiness.

There is no doubt that there are scientific methods of measuring one's happiness at any given moment in time. For example, tracking one's serotonin ("the happiness hormone") levels. Apart from the obvious impracticalities, this method of measuring would have its limitations. It would only tell you your serotonin level and, by extension, your happiness level *at a particular moment in time*. It is not feasible or even possible to spend our lives continuously wired up, recording our serotonin levels. And while it is important to experience regular *moments* of happiness, it is something quite different to a state of general, overall happiness that is not necessarily triggered by a specific event. I call it joy versus contentment.

I'm fortunate enough to start every morning with two moments of immense joy. My two children attend the same school where my wife teaches. A typical day involves me helping to get them ready for school in the morning and bidding them and my wife goodbye before I get ready for my work-from-home day. Now, in recent weeks, my 4-year-old son has started making a point of saying "Have a good day Daddy, I love you." It's just the cutest thing, that absolutely melts my heart. My 6-year-old daughter, never to be outdone of course, will then have to do the same, but with some added embellishment. Those moments make my heart smile. They bring me unbridled joy, every single morning. But that's not all. Those moments would induce the very same feelings within me regardless of any other circumstances of my life. And this should start to demonstrate the distinction. Those moments of joy are priceless. But ultimately, they are merely moments. Fleeting moments, followed by a return to your default setting. It's that default setting that is far more telling. It is your level of contentment and your overall happiness with the state of your life in general, with or without those fleeting moments of joy. This is what I believe can and should be measured, somehow, to produce what I've named *the Happiness Score*.

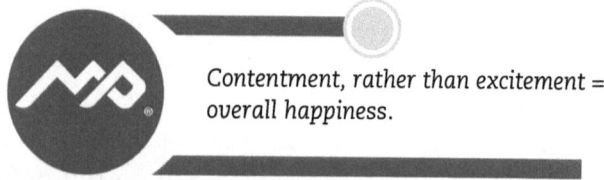

Contentment, rather than excitement = overall happiness.

The Happiness Score *can* be assigned a numerical value, which is critical for any meaningful measurement. To get a measurement, you must know what you're measuring. That sounds obvious, but it isn't really. You cannot measure a person's height if you're not clear on the meaning of the word "height". So, what is the meaning of this thing – *happiness* – which must be measured? Happiness is, quite simply, the absence of stress. And by stress, I mean the broad sense of anything that threatens or detracts from your sense of being at ease.

Happiness is the absence of negative emotions. So, in essence, what is being measured here is how often you experience and, critically, by extension, how often you *don't* experience negative emotions in your day, your week and your month. These emotions would include general sadness, depression, anger, jealousy, fear, anxiety, resentment, frustration and others. You see, happiness is wholly positive. It cannot co-exist with a negative emotion – *any* negative emotion – in the same moment. Determining your level of happiness doesn't require constant tracking of hormonal and neurotransmitter levels or anything remotely as complex. Rather, it just requires a bit of honest introspection to gauge your mood and general mental state over the course of chunks of time that make up your day. If you hate your job and/or your boss, then chances are that most of your 8 to 10-hour workday is characterised by feelings of anger, resentment and frustration. If your marriage is on the rocks, your time at home is likely to be spent in misery. If you live in an unsafe neighbourhood, significant portions of your time at home are spent in a state of fear and anxiety, which will go further to encroach upon your quality of sleep as well. If you're a materialistic person, you'll find yourself experiencing jealousy far too often, and frustration when you can't keep up with every new materialistic trend. The examples are endless, as are the potential stress triggers out there.

> Your Happiness Score = proportion of time spent **without** experiencing negative emotions.

So how do you calculate it? Here's the formula:

$$\frac{\text{Total No. of hours} - \text{Number of hours spent under stress} * 100}{\text{Total number of hours}}$$

Figure 3.1 below shows what a typical day could look like in the life of a formally employed adult, and how to convert it into a Happiness Score.

Time	Activity Description	Stressed (Yes or No)	Hours spent stressed
0600-0630	Woke up late because alarm didn't go off. Rushed to get ready and didn't have breakfast.	Yes	0.5
0630-0730	Terrible traffic. 3 people cut in front of me, which infuriates me! I didn't get to work on time.	Yes	1.0
0730-0800	At work trying to settle down, and wondering if my boss noticed I was late.	Yes	0.5
0800-0900	Settled down and got on with my work.	No	0.0
0900-1100	Ad hoc staff meeting called. I hate meetings; and I don't even think I needed to be in this one; and it's going to put me under serious pressure for other task deadlines.	Yes	2.0

Time	Activity Description	Stressed (Yes or No)	Hours spent stressed
1100-11.30	Frantically trying to re-plan the rest of my day to finish certain tasks.	Yes	0.5
1130-1300	Getting on with tasks I need to get on with. I earned myself a lunch break.	No	0.0
1300-1330	Took a much-needed lunch break and managed to mentally turn off for a while.	No	0.0
1330-1530	Getting on with tasks I need to get on with.	No	0.0
1530-1600	Interruptions from colleagues. I'll now need to work late or take work home.	Yes	0.5
1600-1730	Stuck in traffic. Traffic lights not working.	Yes	1.5
1730-1800	Had a lie down after a hectic day, but the work I brought home is weighing heavily on my mind. So is the fact that I can't go to the gym today; and won't have time to cook either. I'll have to order take out, which I would rather not do.	Yes	0.5

Time	Activity Description	Stressed (Yes or No)	Hours spent stressed
1800-2100	Frantically working (eating while I work). I have such a headache, but this needs to be done.	Yes	3.0
2100	Sleep.		
Hours awake			13.0
Hours stressed			10.0

Fig 3.1 – Breakdown of a typical day

Using the formula above:

$$\frac{(13-10) * 100}{13}$$

$$= \frac{3 * 100}{13}$$

Happiness Score (for that day) = 23%

We could possibly include time spent asleep by gauging the quality and peacefulness of sleep. This is less easy though and requires sophisticated means such as sleep trackers and perhaps input from experts in the field of sleep therapy. But for purposes of this book, it is worth simply pointing out that there is a direct link between happiness and sleep. There is someone I know who went several months with some form of insomnia (undiagnosed). She would spend hours every night trying, largely unsuccessfully, to fall asleep. The underlying issue that was weighing heavily on her mind, and consequently impacting her happiness and in turn her sleep, was a substantial debt she had.

This reminds me of a church sermon I heard a couple of years back from a certain Father Thabo in Johannesburg. It was, and remains, profound. He singled out one specific window of time in our days that we need to pay close attention to. It is that window between the time we lay our heads down on the pillow at night, and the time we fall asleep. What we think about during this timeframe is the thing that is, in Father Thabo's words, "consuming you".

There are triggers that can change your mood just like that, and ultimately lower your happiness score. The critical question is, what do you do about it? You must do something about it because when you reduce the feelings of negative emotion, you increase your general state of contentment, as Fig 3.2 illustrates. That means improving your Happiness Score.

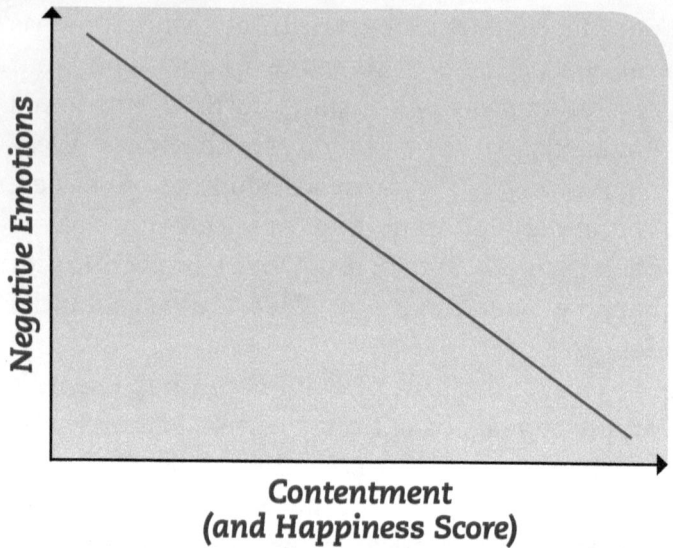

Fig 3.2 – *The impact of negative emotions*

The aim is to eliminate stress from your life, or at least reduce it wherever possible. And believe it or not, this is largely within our control!

CHAPTER 4

MAKE YOURSELF HAPPY

I recently came across a brilliant meme. I'm pretty sure a fair number of readers would have come across it in this age where there is a meme for everything you can think of, and more. It depicts one person holding a box labelled "happiness" and a second person who asks him "Where did you get that? I've been searching for it everywhere." The response is simple and splendid – "I created it myself."

Perhaps over-simplistic at first glance, we really can make ourselves a lot happier just by making a conscious decision to do so. You see, happiness is a concept. It is a concept that manifests itself as a state of mind. Most importantly, though, it is a highly subjective state of mind. It is substantially different from most, if not all, of the things that we enjoy in life. Waking up tomorrow and deciding to be significantly happier than you were yesterday is doable and costs nothing. It is very different from, say, waking up and deciding that you will have 10% less body fat than you had yesterday; or that you will have a few thousand more dollars in your bank account. To reiterate, happiness is just a state of mind.

And controlling our minds is something we can all do. Or at least something we can all *learn* to do *if we chose to*.

As we unpacked in the previous chapter, we all have a Happiness Score. It is essentially the proportion of our time that is spent in a stress-free state. It follows, then, that in order to make ourselves happy (or *happier*), which is to increase our Happiness Score, we need to eliminate stress from our lives. Or at least reduce it. So far, fairly simple.

Things become problematic – or most of us *think* they do – when we consider that stressful situations happen upon us almost daily, with little or no opportunity for us to avoid them. While this may be true, it represents only one side of the coin. The other side of the coin is that many of these unavoidable situations are not actually stressful situations and should not be seen as such. They are merely situations which have the *potential* to become stressful. They are triggers, but what they actually trigger or don't trigger is within our control. When we come to realise this, it becomes much easier to appreciate that when faced with such circumstances, we have not only the opportunity, but also the power to determine the way in which we react. In other words, we can control the extent to which we will allow ourselves to become stressed. In doing so, we are controlling and setting our Happiness Score. We are making ourselves happy (or not).

An easily relatable example is that idiot who

cuts in front of you in rush hour traffic. We all know him, and we all have to deal with him at some point. You instinctively blow your horn and proceed to mutter obscenities under your breath. And what does he do? He pulls the finger at you! The nerve! It is a classic example of one of the many situations that happen upon us with little or no opportunity to avoid them. Or is it? This marks the fork in the road. Not the road you're having to share with this jerk, but the proverbial road that will lead you towards high stress levels if you don't take the other turn very quickly. It is the road towards a certain state of mind for the next few hours. It is the fork in the road that could well impact your Happiness Score for the day. You either allow that incident to worsen your already compromised mood, possibly even going to the extent of trying to pull up beside him and give him a piece of our mind (or your fist); or you simply tell yourself that he's clearly an idiot and he won't be changed by what you say or do, so you will not allow yourself to be subjected to unnecessary stress because of him. The latter is, of course, the preferable choice. As I write this, one of my brother's favourite mantras, which he picked up from the movie Madagascar, comes to mind – "Just smile and wave boys, smile and wave!" In other words, don't allow yourself to be drawn into unnecessary drama and chaos that may be going on around you.

But if we're being honest with ourselves and

practical, as I believe we must be, it is also the more difficult choice. Especially in the heat of the moment. The point here, and the lesson to be learnt, is that it is *possible* to take control of the levels of stress we allow ourselves to experience. That doesn't mean it is easy. It is a skill and, just like any other skill, it must first be learnt (I hope this book and this chapter will help to tick that box); and it must then be mastered through practice. It is not quick or easy, but then again, nothing worthwhile in life ever is. One thing is certain though – it will make you exponentially happier in life.

Then there are the *avoidable* stress triggers. Sticking with the traffic theme, the rush hour traffic and the possibility of being late for work undoubtedly brings on a certain level of stress. But unlike the previous example, it may be irresponsible to simply decide *not* to be stressed by the fact that you are likely to be late for work. There are consequences that will have to be faced, and those consequences cannot be magically wished away in the interest of boosting your Happiness Score. The better solution, then, is not in *your mind*. It is in *your actions*. The key word here – whether in respect of the mind or the actions – is that they are *yours*! Ensure that you get up, get ready and leave the house 15 minutes earlier to avoid the stress presented by the prospect of being late for work *again*. There is so much unnecessary stress that we invite upon ourselves in life, purely because we refuse to do certain things. We refuse to develop good habits. Small and easy ones, but good and valuable ones. This routine refusal is born of laziness and lack of self-discipline. Well, I guess the latter falls within the scope of the former. Lack of self-discipline is essentially mental laziness.

These examples, and more importantly the principle of two categories of stress triggers – unavoidable and avoidable – are illustrated in the flow chart shown in fig 4.1 below.

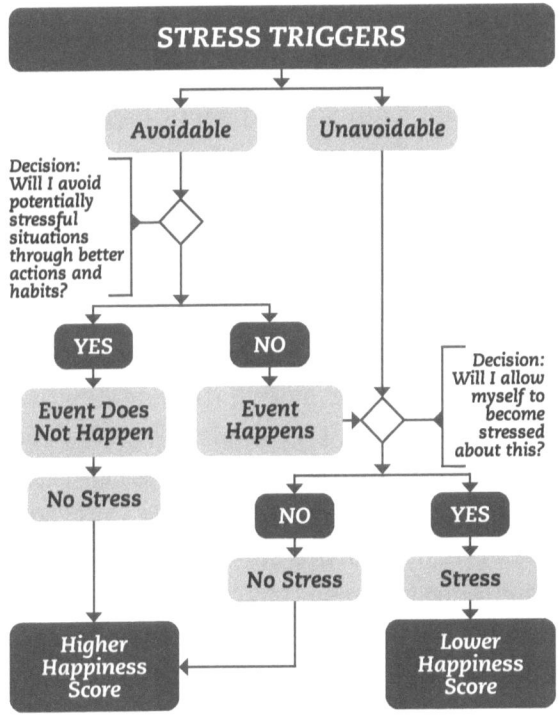

Fig 4.1 Stress triggers and their possible impacts

If we train ourselves to see these potentially stressful situations this way, we will immediately increase our Happiness Scores. And the best part, as you will have seen from Fig 4.1, is that you get two bites at the cherry:

- You can decide to take actions and form habits that will avoid a potential stressful situation; or, if that fails, (or if the situation is genuinely unavoidable)
- You still get to choose the way you react. The way you allow this stress trigger to affect you... or *not* affect you!

This flow chart should visually clarify the important point that even *after* an event has happened, whether it was avoidable or not, it remains only a *potentially* stressful event. You still have the power to decide what happens next. Do you become stressed or not? It's your call.

I thought twice, and then a third and fourth time, about whether to share this example about my wife. Well, here goes... (I'll deal with the consequences when she reads this). We have a designated spot for the car key. It is right next to the front door of our apartment. The "rule" is that whoever has driven the car must put the key in its designated spot as soon as they walk in. Easy to do; easy to understand; and easy to see the value in the rule. Yet my wife does it only four or five times out of ten. What this means is that five or six out of ten times, when she wants to leave (which is, more often than not, with no time to spare, and understandably so when there are two young children in tow), she gets to the door only to realise that the car key is not there. She was already stressed because she was cutting things fine (which, itself, could have been avoided); and her stress levels have now escalated because she can't leave. She must look for the key. Is it in her handbag? Oh, wait, she didn't use this handbag when she went out yesterday. Where's the other handbag? Which one was it? Oh dear ... where is this key!?

Developing good habits, even small ones, significantly reduces stress and consequently makes you happier! While it is doable to re-programme our minds to not react to the idiot driver every morning, it is far easier to form a better habit like getting up and leaving 15 minutes earlier to avoid the chaotic traffic and, in so doing, significantly reduce the chances of that guy cutting in front of you. And if he still does, well, you're 15 minutes ahead of schedule so it's not going to make you late. Smile and wave!

As always, we must be practical and realistic, and Charles Duhigg[4] shares some sound advice:

> "It is important to note that though the process of habit change is easily described, it does not necessarily follow that it is easily accomplished. It is facile to imply that smoking, alcoholism, over-eating, or other

ingrained patterns can be upended without real effort. Genuine change requires work and self-understanding of the cravings driving behaviours. Changing any habit requires determination."

Duhigg[5] goes on to recount William James's view that:

"All our life, so far as it has definite form, is but a mass of habits – practical, emotional, and intellectual – systematically organized for our weal or woe, and bearing us irresistibly toward our destiny, whatever the latter may be."

There is another monster, far bigger and far more dangerous, that we not only live with but invite into our lives. It is the stress we routinely bring upon ourselves because of the things we *don't have*. There are things that we need to have in life – food, shelter, clothing and other items to meet our needs. Without those, stress is not only inevitable, but also necessary. That is perhaps the primary purpose of stress – to scare ourselves into action when action is required for survival. But that is not the category of "things" I'm referring to. It is the things that we don't have, but don't *need* to have either. The things that satisfy our often irrational and downright silly desires. It is this category that brings untold, but all completely unnecessary, stress and misery to millions upon millions of people. We're all guilty of this on varying levels, especially in these unfortunate times dominated by social media, materialism and consumerism. We routinely and foolishly make ourselves stressed and miserable trying to impress people who mean little in the grander scheme of our lives. Unlike the douchebag driver that you will unavoidably encounter from time to time, the way we feel about and react towards material things is a purely internal trigger. There is no doubt social media and various aspects of life – like seeing the fancy new car in your neighbour's driveway or hearing about your colleague's exotic holiday – can easily illicit feelings of jealousy and inadequacy. But – and it's a big *but* – only if we allow it to. We will look at this in more detail in the coming chapters.

In case you hadn't noticed, the way we react – the way we *choose* to react – to internal triggers also forms part of habit. To an extent, we are the sum of our habits. If you want a better life – a happier life – start by looking at your habits, and then changing them as required. I shall close this chapter with a profound quote from Mathias Alexander:

"*People do not decide their future, they decide their habits and their habits decide their future.*"

CHAPTER 5

HAPPINESS v PLEASURE

Well, what's the difference? Is there a difference in the first place? Many of us don't see or make any distinction between happiness and pleasure in everyday life. The result is that we find ourselves mindlessly chasing every cheap (or expensive) pleasure we can on the assumption that more pleasure, surely, equals more happiness. It doesn't! In fact, it can be quite the opposite.

I should, perhaps, start by looking into the science behind this distinction. And there is science.

Let's ease into it by looking at two simple workouts in the gym. The first is a steady, medium paced run on the treadmill for an hour; and the second is a one-hour heavy weight-lifting session. On the face of things, even for a person who is not performing these workouts or never has, it is patently clear that the body, whilst clearly working in both cases, is working very *differently* in each workout. Without knowing or understanding the biology behind it, I would go as far as saying it is unanimously accepted that a one-hour run is quite different to a one-hour weights session.

The difference, which is easily acceptable at face value, finds its explanation in the systems of the human body. The systems primarily at work during these respective training sessions are the same – cardiovascular and musculoskeletal. And for this reason, they fall under the same broad category called *physical exercise*. The way these systems are working is where the difference lies. Different energy pathways, different heart rates, different breathing, different movements, different muscle fibres, and different muscular exertion among others. Most of these differences can be seen by an observer and felt by the person doing the exercises. But still, it is the same systems within the human body that are at work.

The same principle applies to happiness and pleasure. The same systems are primarily at play – the endocrine system, which produces and releases various hormones and chemicals; and the nervous system, which uses them in various ways. Thus, these two feelings of happiness and pleasure, just like the two different gym workouts, plausibly fall under the same broad category. We might call this category *feeling good*. Because they share a particular category and because of the obvious similarities, the feelings of happiness and pleasure are routinely, but of course erroneously, lumped together as one and the same thing.

Let's look closer: The feeling of happiness is induced by the release of the chemical serotonin, while the feeling of pleasure is triggered by the release of the chemical dopamine. To produce, release and use these two respective chemicals, it follows that the responsible systems of the human body must be doing two different things. They are working in different ways when we're experiencing happiness as compared to when we are experiencing pleasure.

It is, perhaps, a case of seeing is believing. We are all doubting Thomases on some level. We can easily *see* the differences in the way the cardiovascular and musculoskeletal systems are working during different exercise routines, so, by virtue of seeing, we believe and even know that they are different. By contrast, we cannot see the endocrine and nervous systems and what they are doing, but we must, nevertheless, trust that they are doing different things which render happiness and pleasure separate and distinct from each other. This can be difficult.

One of the biggest established differentiating factors is that happiness can only exist in a state of safety[6], while pleasure can exist in a state of safety or threat. Think of skydiving or driving a performance car at 200km per hour. These activities have their attraction, of course, but we know on some level that they're not the steps to happiness. We know – before, during and after the act – that we're getting something other than happiness from the act in question.

Serotonin, commonly known as "the happiness hormone", is released through natural healthy activities: eating a balanced diet, exercising and getting sunlight. Dopamine, which induces the feeling of pleasure, is quite different. While it is improved through diet, it is released mainly in response to external triggers; things that make the brain anticipate a reward and then, of course, the actual receipt of the anticipated reward. Common examples would be eating or even smelling certain foods, going shopping, sex, or taking recreational drugs. When we perform these acts, dopamine is released, and it feels good. For a while. We want to do the same thing again, and again, because the brain remembers how it made us feel good and, naturally, we want to re-live that pleasure.

Here we begin to see another critical difference. Perhaps *the* critical difference which is also more easily relatable than a biology lesson on the systems of the human body. Happiness comes from within; from the situation prevailing in your life at a given time. From your baseline reality. It is your day-to-day norm, or your default setting that we touched on in chapter 2. Pleasure, by contrast, comes from external sources that we go looking for, in most cases in a bid to improve our day-to-day norm.

It follows then that the more you find yourself actively looking for short-lived pleasures, the less satisfied you probably are with your day-to-day norm. And, consequently, the less happy you probably are. Rather than seeking short-term pleasure after short-term pleasure, the better solution is to carry out an honest – perhaps brutally honest – self-interrogation into what might be missing from your day-to-day norm. What are the gaps that you are trying to fill through pleasure-seeking? The distinction between happiness and pleasure goes hand in hand with another critical distinction – that between needs and desires. We look at the latter in more detail in chapter 7.

Let's look at another obvious, but more ominous example of pleasure-seeking and its adverse effects – taking recreational drugs. Putting aside the first time, which may be the result of peer pressure, simple curiosity or any number of things, the reality is that anyone who takes recreational drugs does so for one reason and one reason only (whether there is an addiction attached to it or not). The reason is pleasure. The pleasurable feeling – the high – that they get in the immediate aftermath. But that high doesn't last forever. It doesn't even last long. Sooner or later normal settings are restored, and this person is returned to "real life". That drug-induced high has not, magically, taken away the huge debt you have, the boss that makes your life a misery, the daily anxiety induced by living in an unsafe neighbourhood, the health concerns you or your family members have ... and the list goes on. All these concerns that you have in real life negatively impact your happiness score for most of the day, the week, the month. That drug-induced high may improve your happiness score over the period of an hour, but it certainly will not do that over the course of a day or a week. In fact, in the grander scheme of things, it will reduce your happiness score. When you are not under the influence of drugs, you will come to realise that you have another problem – this drug habit – to add to the existing list of problems that you were trying to escape in the first place. The debt, the douchebag boss, and so on. It cannot be overemphasized: happiness comes from within, while pleasure is dependent upon sources that we go out looking for in an often-futile attempt to improve our day-to-day norm. The reality is that all we really achieve through compulsive pleasure-seeking is to temporarily forget the things we don't want to face, but ultimately still must.

The well-known story of Angie Bachmann represents a perfect illustration of the insidious nature of pleasures. Duhigg[7] provides a perfect introduction to Bachmann's story, that I need not tamper with:

> "The morning the trouble began – years before she realized there was even trouble in the first place – Angie Bachmann was sitting at home, staring at the television, so bored that she was giving serious thought to reorganizing the silverware drawer.
>
> Her youngest daughter had started kindergarten a few weeks earlier and her two older daughters were in middle school, their lives filled with friends and activities and gossip their mother couldn't possibly understand. Her husband, a land surveyor, often left work at eight and didn't get home until six. The

house was empty except for Bachmann. It was the first time in almost two decades – since she had gotten married at nineteen and pregnant by twenty, and her days had become crowded with packing school lunches, playing princess and running a family shuttle service – that she felt genuinely alone. Now it was ten thirty in the morning, her three daughters were gone, and Bachmann had resorted – again – to taping a piece of paper over the kitchen clock to stop herself from looking at it every three minutes.

That day, she made a deal with herself: If she could make it until noon without going crazy or eating the cake in the fridge, she would leave the house and do something fun. She spent the next ninety minutes trying to figure out what exactly that would be. When the clock hit twelve o'clock, she put on some makeup and a nice dress and drove to riverboat casino about twenty minutes away from her house. Even at noon on a Thursday, the casino was filled with people doing things besides watching soap operas and folding the laundry. There was a band playing near the entrance. A woman was handing out free cocktails. Bachman ate shrimp from a buffet. The whole experience felt luxurious."

To cut to the chase, if you don't know this infamous story already, Bachman became heavily addicted to gambling and in a matter of years was declared bankrupt. As luck would have it, a couple of years after she was declared bankrupt, she inherited a million dollars from her father. Sure enough, it was just a matter of time before that entire inheritance had been gambled away.

The moral of the story is that even the most innocent looking, small, controllable pleasures can grow into the most unmanageable, life-changing addictions. Angie Bachmann, as the story goes, had actually set herself stringent rules at the beginning, by which she strictly abided (at first). Only once a week; only one hour per visit; and only using cash she had in her purse. But as the addiction grew, the rules quickly flew out of the window.

There is an old adage, "everything in moderation". An educated guess tells me that it was coined with specific reference to many of life's pleasures. Not all pleasures have to represent such negativity as drug or gambling addictions. By all means treat yourself to some of life's pleasures from time to time. They are as necessary as they are pleasing, for they serve to take the edge off the oft monotonous and draining obligations that life throws up.

The trick is not to allow pleasures to become compulsive and addictive; and, most importantly, make sure not to confuse them for happiness.

CHAPTER 6

NOSTALGIA

As I set about the next part of this book I was reminded of a certain, not inexpensive, pair of trainers that I recently bought. And I began to ponder whether I had practiced what I was about to preach, in particular the folly of materialism and the evils of consumerism. I immediately knew there was something different about this purchase. I knew it at the time of the purchase, and I knew it as I was writing. But I couldn't quite put my finger on *what* was different. Or was I just rationalising away this spontaneous, unnecessary and somewhat extravagant purchase?

As I contemplated further, I did eventually manage to put my finger on it. There is this extraordinary category of things that we do, which is driven neither by basic need nor by the desire to impress others (as so many desires are). This category indices the feeling – the very special feeling – of nostalgia. So much so, that after having finally managed to put my finger on it, I was constrained to come back and add another chapter – this chapter – before moving on to Part III. From time to time, life will present the opportunity to do or to acquire things that have the effect of mentally transporting us back in time. Back to happy days and special times. To re-live fond memories. Take those opportunities when they arise. They don't seem to follow logic, and nor should they. But I assure you, they will make you happy.

    And so, back to my new trainers. I was visiting my brother in Johannesburg for a weekend. I took him and his family out for breakfast after church on Sunday, after which he decided it was a good opportunity to do a bit of grocery shopping (insert eye-roll emoji). This wasn't really what I wanted to be doing, but I soon realised that it happened for a reason, as I believe does everything. I wandered around the grocery store with them for a while, before going off to find the public bathroom as this grocery store visit didn't seem to be ending any time soon. On my way I came across a small and inconspicuous sports store. Not one of the major franchise stores, and not one that I had ever noticed before, despite frequenting this particular shopping centre each time I visited Johannesburg. There, staring at me from the shop window, beckoning to me, was a pair of Allen Iverson "Question" sneakers. They were classics. They *are* classics. These are the sneakers that Iverson was wearing when, in his barnstorming rookie NBA season, he infamously crossed over the great(est?) Michael Jordan. They immediately took me back to 1997, the year they first made an appearance in Zimbabwe, after their 1996 official release in the United Sates. As a 17-year-old back then, I didn't have the privilege of owning a pair. I was at the mercy of my parents and their financial constraints which, in hindsight, I didn't come close to appreciating at the time. A couple of my school friends were more fortunate than I was. I loved those sneakers. I coveted them. I yearned for them. But I never got them. Now there's been a re-release to commemorate the 25th anniversary of this iconic shoe and the NBA debut of this iconic player. I simply had to get them ... or did I? An internal battle ensued. It was my pragmatic self against that 17-year-old that still lurks somewhere within me. As it often does in these instances, the former prevailed.

The first battle was over, but that internal war was not. Those sneakers weighed heavily on my mind for the remainder of that day, and the following day. Not for what they inherently *were*, but for what they represented. Two days later – the day I was leaving Johannesburg – that 17-year-old inside me prevailed. I convinced my brother to stop by that store on the way to the airport and I bought the sneakers. I simply had to have them. And I did!

1997 and 1998 were my sixth form years at school. In many respects, they remain the two best years of my life. These sneakers served to exhume and illuminate all those neurological pathways that had been buried somewhere in my brain decades ago. And with them, all the warm and fuzzy feelings of a period in my life laden with magical memories. And this process is repeated each time I put on this pair of sneakers. They bring me pure, unadulterated happiness. I posted a picture of them on Facebook soon after. It wasn't to be boastful but, rather, to see who would recognize them. My post was a hit, just like the sneakers themselves were 25 years previously. Comments came flooding in, predominantly from my high-school mates. The beauty of it was that there we were all in our own corners of the world, but together re-living our fond high school memories, decades later. There were comments from people I had not been in touch with for over ten years. We all reconnected on some level. We were all transported, momentarily, back to 1997. It was an amazing feeling!

Be on the lookout for these nostalgia inducers. They can be shoes (like mine), clothes, smells, places. Buy a bottle of that perfume you wore on your wedding day. The one that, perhaps, trumps all others is to take your children to places that hold fond memories from your own childhood, and relive those memories vicariously.

My parents were divorced before I was old enough to remember anything. But for my sister and I, all the negativity of the divorce was offset several times over by relationships that we developed with our paternal grandparents. They were the perfect grandparents – spoiling us; and having far more patience with us than our parents did; and doing all the "grandparent stuff". But each time I reflect, I realise more and more how they were, in so many respects, a second set of parents to my sister and me. And as much as I love my own parents, my grandparents were better parents to us than they were, in so many ways. And, of course, they showed us that marriage *could* last for over 50 years, "til death do us part", and didn't have to end the way our parents' did.

Growing up we spent so much time at their house, playing in their garden, feeding the tortoises, climbing the huge avocado tree and all sorts. It is a house that holds timeless and priceless memories. My grandfather built it himself in the 1950s and extended it in the 1980s. During the extension, my sister and I would play in the foundations over weekends, telling ourselves and anyone who would listen that we were "helping" my grandfather with the building work. What we were really doing was making a mess with the wet cement, and probably getting in my grandfather's way. He never let on. He always made us feel like we really were helping; like we actually had a constructive hand in building that house.

My grandmother died when I was 19 years old and my grandfather, to the surprise of almost everyone in the family, pushed on for another 18 years despite having suffered two heart attacks even before his wife died. They're both gone now, but my aunt – my late father's sister – still lives in that house. That house that was built by my grandfather (ably assisted by my sister and me, of course). It is now, legally, my aunt's house, but it will forever be "my grandparents' house". Because it remains in the family, I can take my own children there to feed the same tortoises, play in the same garden and hide behind the same rockery that I did. They play with the very same (perhaps antiquated) toys that my sister and I played with decades ago. And as I watch them, I get the distinct sense that I am watching my sister and myself, some 35 years ago, as I relive the myriads of precious memories. It makes my heart smile. It's absolute magic!

Psychology writer Alfred Mander[8] lists what he calls 13 "originating instincts" in every person and goes on to say that these originating instincts become "wants" and, throughout our lives – whether consciously or subconsciously – we seek to satisfy them. There is one particular originating instinct that stands out from Mander's list: to return to what is familiar. I've singled this one out because it is unique. Unlike any other, you see, its most integral component is the past. *Your* past. Your *unique* past. To satisfy the wants that stem from this instinct, we need to return – whether physically or mentally – to people, places, things or conditions that we have already experienced in the past. Unlike, for example, the originating instinct to seek companionship, in which we seek out someone suitable, often through years of trial and error, with whom we can not only share a future, but shape one together. But we don't get to shape what we're going back to. Our options are limited. Limited by our own distinct past.

I could have bought any one of a dozen new pairs of sneakers in that small sports store in Johannesburg, and they would probably have made me feel good in some way. They would have given me that hit of dopamine that retail therapy invariably does. But none of them would have had, and continue to have, the effect of taking me back to my high school years. I can, and do, watch my children playing in so many different places, and it makes me happy every time. But it seldom takes me back to my own childhood the way it does when I watch them play at my grandparents' house.

But while we are limited by our past, that doesn't stop life from doing its best to continually present us with opportunities to relive happy times of years gone by. We need only to be on better look out for them. And then grab them! And if life is not placing those 1996 Allen Iverson sneakers in the shop window that you're walking past, make your own nostalgic moments for yourself. Pull out those old photo albums; look for the top 10 music hits from one of your teenage years; or take a trip to a place you loved the first time you visited it.

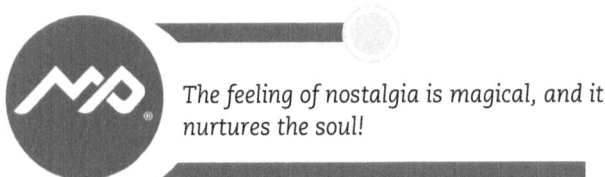

The feeling of nostalgia is magical, and it nurtures the soul!

PART III
PEOPLE

CHAPTER 7

NEEDS AND DESIRES

Human beings, just like any other living species, are primarily driven by a common set of inherent needs; things that are necessary for survival – survival of self and species. We differ greatly, however, from all other species when it comes to desires. The extent to which we are driven by certain desires has the potential to cause so much misery and suffering to humanity. The worst of it all, is that these desires are so often things that we don't really need, and that we *know* we don't really need.

Before going any further, I should hasten to point out that desires and the motivation to achieve them are not inherently bad. Not by any means. If we didn't have them and were not motivated by them, human beings would have stagnated in the stone age, "happily" hunting, gathering and (barely) meeting our needs from day to day. Desires need not be frowned upon in wholesale fashion. It's more a case of managing those desires and setting parameters within which they should be pursued. These parameters are summed up pretty well by what our conscience tells us. The voice of the ego, which drives the pursuit of materialistic desires, should never drown out the voice of the conscience. But that takes us on a tangent that deviates away from individual happiness and what we can do for ourselves rather than for humanity as a whole. The point, rather – and it is a critical one in the context of this book – is that there is a distinction between needs and desires, and it is a distinction we need to be consciously aware of in the quest for happiness.

There is no better authority on the topic than Maslow, and in particular his hierarchy of human needs and desires. It provides a blueprint on what drives and motivates human beings in whatever we do and is illustrated in figure 5.1 below.

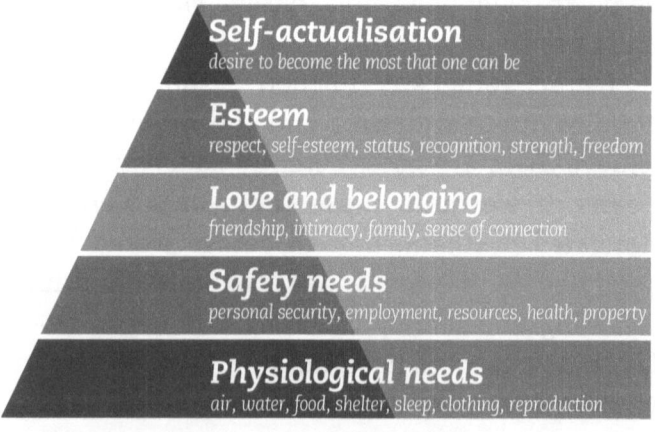

Fig. 7.1 Maslow's Hierarchy of Human Needs
Source: Maslow, AH. 'A Theory of Human Motivation'. *Psychological Review* 50(4) 370–96 (1943)

This illustration makes the critical distinction between needs and desires easier to decode. In essence, the bottom three tiers constitute needs – physiological, safety and belonging.

If we look back at chapter 4, I spoke about the stress we invite upon ourselves because of what we don't have. And I categorised these things into those that we don't have but need to have; and those that we don't have and don't need to have either. It should now be obvious that these two categories are, essentially, needs and desires respectively.

And while the message in that chapter – "make yourself happy" – is, indeed highly applicable in day-to-day life, it is also a message that can easily come across as over-simplistic and idealistic. The ability to truly make ourselves happier in general is, admittedly, circumstantial. The set of circumstances upon which it is dependant is the satisfaction of our needs. A baseline if you will.

Choosing not to get annoyed by the idiot driver on your way to work is not, in the grander scheme of things, going to make your life significantly better or, more pertinently, significantly *happier*, if you haven't received your pay cheque for three months and you can't pay the rent or feed yourself and your family.

Our needs must be met in order for us to have any decent quality of life, or life at all! This is the non-negotiable foundation upon which happiness is built. If these needs cannot or are not being met then, no matter how hard we may try, we will not be in a state of contentment or happiness. This is a simple fact of life, like it or not. And yes, to address the elephant that has now planted itself in the room, meeting many of these needs *does* require money. As much as we might like to, we can't get away from the necessity of money, within limits, of course. We look at this more in Part IV. For now, suffice to say that if you have the means to have purchased this book, I'm taking the assumption that you are one of the more fortunate ones in the world that is in the financial position to meet your needs. That you have the necessary foundation upon which to build your happiness. And that you *can be* significantly happier in life, just by deciding to be precisely that.

Beyond these needs that form the baseline required for a happy life, lie desires. As I write that I'm taken back to a scene from the Lion King, in which Mufasa is shown pointing out the extent of his kingdom to young Simba, and the shadows that lie beyond. The shadows where the hyenas prowl. The shadows into which Simba must never venture (which, of course, he does). Our happiness is too often sabotaged by these desires. They can very easily become those hyenas that lurk in the shadows beyond, threatening young Simba's life. But when we equip ourselves with the ability to clearly distinguish between needs and desires, we take a giant step towards developing the ability to avoid the trap that these desires routinely set without our conscious knowledge.

Desires are represented in the second-from-top tier of Maslow's hierarchy – self-esteem. Desires may manifest themselves in many forms but these, ultimately, form the category of things that we chase after without *needing* to. This is where we all fall into the Trap. The mental trap which sees us adopting, almost by default, the attitude that we simply *must* have certain material things. Our minds, often subconsciously, have a habit of somehow converting these material things from desires to needs. This conversion, of course, takes place only in our minds. In reality, desires remain desires. These are the things whose absence causes us so much stress and, consequently, lowers our Happiness Score. But only because we allow it to. It doesn't have to be that way!

I should say a few words about self-actualisation, which forms the top tier of Maslow's hierarchy. This tier is labelled in a somewhat misleading manner – "desire to become the most one can be". Despite the wording, I believe that self-actualisation is not a *desire* per se, but rather the drive to find and live out one's purpose. I do believe that it is the ultimate success in life, and we should all aim first to uncover it, and then to attain it. I speak about this at length in *Life Demystified*, and unpack it further in Part V. The manner in which we pursue self-actualisation is critical. The two – self actualisation or purpose, and happiness – should form a complimentary rather than antagonistic pair. Self-actualisation must be pursued in a manner that is consistent with day-to-day happiness. Pursuing the former should not be at the expense of the latter, otherwise it becomes a self-defeating process, and the inevitable result is added stress. This, as we know, means a lowered Happiness Score.

It is the desire for status that is the most damaging. It is one that we try to attain through the acquisition and parading of material things. Expensive ones. The erroneous assumption is that the more I can flaunt, the more successful I will be perceived by anyone who sees me. And the more successful I am perceived to be, the happier I will be. But, unlike good health for example, which is objectively beneficial to everybody, material things that extend beyond your needs are of no objective benefit. Pursuing and acquiring them will not make you happy. For if you are that way inclined, it will only make you start yearning for the better model that you now don't have. And that is how so many global brands survive and thrive; constantly releasing the newer models and playing on the weak minds of consumers who simply *must* have every new model as soon as it is released. I mean, honestly, how can people sleep outside a store overnight just so that they can be one of the first people to pay $1000 for a phone that is just negligibly "better" than the one they paid

$1000 for less than 12 months ago? You remain in a constant state of dissatisfaction. Not having those things, however, doesn't have to make you unhappy. If you can only reconfigure your mindset to the reality that nobody worthwhile actually cares about your material possessions, you will become a lot more content. A lot happier. And that is the reality. Nobody worthwhile cares about your material possessions. This is consistent with Socrates' philosophy:

"The secret of happiness, you see, is not found in seeking more but in developing the capacity to enjoy less"

CHAPTER 8

WHO ARE YOU TRYING TO IMPRESS?

> Nobody worthwhile cares about your material possessions!

Let that sink in! If there is only one lesson you take out of this book, this should probably be it. Think about this the next time you set about trying to impress somebody, particularly with material things.

The important relationships that exist in life are those we have with our parents, grandparents, siblings, spouse/partner, children, and *real* friends. These are the people that matter. And these are the people who will not be coerced into liking us or loving us more (or at all) because of our material possessions. (The obvious exception is a partner/spouse, many of whom, in this age of ultra-materialism, trade their "love" and affection for material gain. But that category of spouse/partner presents an entirely different conundrum for a different time.) In fact, attempts to impress people through materialism have the uncanny ability to achieve the opposite. While you may succeed in the short term in impressing certain people, these are the people that will add nothing meaningful to your life. The people who matter become alienated. These are the ones who can see the changes in our behaviour; the negative changes that are occasioned by increased materialism and our desire to impress relative strangers in a bid to give ourselves some perceived higher status.

> If you can't look back at your younger self and realise that you were an idiot, you're probably still an idiot.

This is a quote of unknown origin I recently came across. I've been doing a lot of that lately! Looking back on my youth and sometimes laughing; sometimes cringing; often both, at the idiocy of my thoughts and actions. Most notably when it came to materialism and the attempts to impress people. Unimportant people! Buying clothing with designer labels brandished as conspicuously as possible for the world to see. As if that made me important. Or as if that even made other people think I was important, which, ridiculously, I assumed it did.

There are so many levels of absurdity to this sort of behaviour. As a starting point, I was a teenager and still at school. I didn't earn money of my own. Everyone who knew me knew this fact. And anyone who didn't know me could guess my age and stage of life. Whatever I was wearing was not bought with *my* money. I had none! When you dumb it down, I was using my parents hard-earned money, not mine, to buy designer label clothes, and I thought it had some bearing on *my* status and importance.

This practice continued into my young adult life. While I could perhaps start taking credit for earning my own money to buy these designer clothes, the second aspect of absurdity was still very much at the fore. I was essentially buying a very basic t-shirt, for example, which probably cost a dollar to manufacture, but I was paying – and happily so – $30 or $40, purely because it had some well-known logo brandished across it. Aside from the fact that it's a rip-off (there will no doubt be arguments about the value of brands and intellectual property blah blah blah) what this means, if you take a bit of time to think about it, is that I made myself a walking billboard for these brands, promoting and advertising them wherever I went. But worst of all, I was paying them for the "privilege" of advertising for them. That is the reality of the situation. And this is what so many people mindlessly do. The question is, who are you trying to impress? Does a t-shirt with a brand name across the front make you more important? Does it make you feel happy?

And here is the summary of many of our lives: we buy things and perform actions that we really don't need to. And that we really can't afford to either. But we do so anyway, purely in a bid to impress people that mean nothing to us. For some warped reason, we take pleasure out of the looks of approval we get from the stranger at the traffic light when we're in our new car. Or the nameless faces in the mall who notice that designer t-shirt we're wearing, or the designer handbag we're proudly carrying. And the truth of the matter – a truth that we're all very well aware of – is that we'll probably never see these strangers again. But somehow we feel good because they noticed us for that fleeting moment. We feel important! Beneath the surface, the rationale is that when we are seen wearing a designer t-shirt, the people – the strangers – who see us will instantaneously and automatically deduce that we are financially successful, because everyone knows that the brand we're proudly brandishing and freely advertising is expensive. And if these strangers think we are financially successful, we feel a sense of importance. That sense of importance boosts our status and esteem. And that, we somehow think, will make us happy.

We can't forget about those infamous Joneses; the ones with whom we mindlessly try to keep up. My neighbour buys a new car, so I must do the same. My work colleague went on an exotic holiday and came back with fantastic stories to tell everyone in the office. I must do the same! After all, I'm in a more senior position than him anyway, so I can't be outdone like that. This is a ridiculous mindset. Get out of it! Here's something to think about from Napoleon Hill's *Think and Grow Rich*:[9]

> "The majority of people who fail to accumulate money sufficient for their needs are, generally, easily influenced by the opinions of others. They permit the newspapers and the gossiping neighbours to do their thinking for them."

And then you get social media. On any given day, you will find several of your "friends" posting about the dinner they had at the fancy new restaurant or the holiday they're on, or pretty much anything they think will impress their social media following. Let's face it ... to a large extent the essence of social media is showing off. To try and convince the world and, perhaps even more so yourself, that you're "doing well". That you're financially successful and, by consequence, you're happy. The things we see on social media can easily, and do regularly, illicit feelings of jealousy and inadequacy. This causes stress which, as we know, lowers our Happiness Score. But here's the thing... the value you attach to the fancy dinners and holidays you see being flaunted on social media by your "friends" is 100% your decision and within your control. Equally importantly, we can change the way we react to these feelings of jealousy and inadequacy. It falls within the scope of application of the Figure 4.1 in chapter 4. We can, and probably should, also change the way we view our own fancy dinners and holidays. The fact that we are throwing them in the face of our social media "friends" as frequently as we can, will never make us happy.

Social media has created a situation where people are so intent and so focused on taking selfies wherever they go. The more beautiful and more exotic the location, the more critical the selfie is. The most important thing, seemingly, is to have the perfect photograph to post on social media. And to post it immediately. And for what? To show it off. Everyone must see that I'm on holiday and, more importantly, that I am (financially) successful enough to be on this holiday. And after that, I will anxiously check every 30 seconds to see how many people have liked and commented on that photo. The more likes and comments I get, the more people know how (financially) successful I am, and therefore the more important I am! This, in turn, will automatically make me happier.

Not only is this plain wrong, but it's also just silly! Not to mention the fact that you will then become very disgruntled when the post doesn't garner the likes and comments that you had anticipated and hoped for. This, of course, reduces your Happiness Score.

This takes me back over 15 years, to what I might call "the good old days". When my wife and I were still dating, we'd go up into the mountains of the beautiful Eastern Highlands of Zimbabwe often, alternating between the two equally beautiful resort towns of Vumba and Nyanga. We would stay at the Leopard Rock Hotel and Troutbeck Inn respectively. They each carried their own distinct charms, and drew equal attraction, but for different reasons. Leopard Rock, modelled on an old French chateau, had its marble floors and glittering chandeliers adorning the reception. It boasted grandeur and grace fit for royalty. Literally. Among the hotel's distinguished guests of years gone by are several members of the British Royal Family. Troutbeck, by contrast, was cosy and quaint with a roaring fire to welcome you in the homely, carpeted lobby.

Another very noticeable difference was that, unlike Troutbeck and despite its opulence, there was no mobile network signal at Leopard Rock. None whatsoever. From the time we arrived until the time we got home our mobile phones were rendered useless. Wi-Fi was something very few people used in Zimbabwe at the time, as were smartphones, so it mattered not. If we needed to reach someone or be reached, the telephone in the hotel room served the purpose. And those little holidays were magic! We took in the splendour of the mountainous terrain, with unparalleled views and majesty. One of the holes on the hotel golf course, as it is most aptly named, gives you the "world's view" across into Mozambique for what looks like hundreds of miles to the horizon. This is where I proposed to my wife on one of these magical trips of ours. After a round of golf we would sit at the clubhouse overlooking the picturesque signature 9th hole with the green planted in the middle of a small, serene lake, with the auburn sun sinking behind the mountains that formed the backdrop. No phones, no social media. Just us and the splendour of nature before us. Which was specifically what we had gone there for. In a word, we were happy! And as I write this, the obvious question is "Where did we go wrong?" And by "we", I don't just mean my wife and me. I mean human beings.

What happens when we're on holiday now – we, human beings – is that we completely miss the opportunity to be physically and mentally present in the moment. To sit down, relax, and fully take in the magnificence of our surroundings – that stunning sunset and the majestic surrounds of this holiday destination that we've planned out for months and anticipated so much. To be completely at peace, for days on end. That, my friends, is happiness. And I'd like to assume that, on some level, that must have been the primary purpose of the holiday, right? But we routinely trade that for the opportunity to show off to the social media minions, whose opinions don't really mean anything in the grander scheme of our lives.

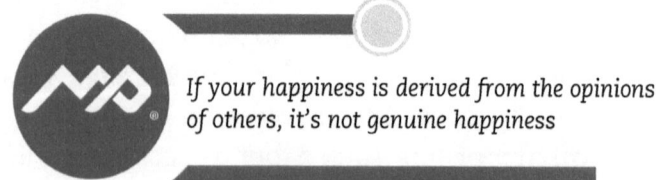

If your happiness is derived from the opinions of others, it's not genuine happiness

CHAPTER 9

IMPRESS YOURSELF!

Having made the distinction between needs and desires, and having shared the value of focusing on the things you *do* have rather than those you *don't*, there is still an elephant in the room. It is the latent implication that we should, perhaps, remain perpetually satisfied with what we have, to the extent that we must remain stagnant in life. Am I suggesting that we be content to never go on holiday, because it is not a need? Must we be satisfied with the same car for 30 years, lest we be accused of trying to keep up with the Joneses? To be clear, I am not implying or suggesting anything of the sort.

Have desires and, more importantly, have dreams that extend beyond your basic needs. Set goals to achieve them. Formulate plans and work on those plans diligently and consistently. However, there are parameters within which goals and dreams must be pursued, and the starting point is being thankful.

As you work towards achieving your goals always remain consciously thankful, not only for the things that you do have, but also for the fact that you have identified the things that you want to attain and are actively working on attaining them. Rather than reminding yourself that you can't afford that dream holiday or that new car right now, tell yourself that in 12 months' time (or whatever time frame you have set for yourself) you will. The former will illicit negative emotions while the latter will illicit positive ones. The former will lower your Happiness Score and the latter will increase it.

INTERROGATE YOUR MOTIVATION

Interrogate the motivation behind your goals and keep interrogating it. Goals aimed at meeting your needs, or meeting your needs *better* are good and necessary. As we know from chapter 7, needs must be met. That is non-negotiable. This is the minimum requirement for happiness. Desires, however, and the goals aimed at fulfilling them, are a different kettle of fish. The motivation for such goals will generally fall into one of two categories:

- To improve the quality of life of myself and/or my family; or
- To meet societal expectations or to impress people.

If it is the first category, get cracking. If it is the second, stop in your tracks and re-think things.

This is illustrated in Fig 9.1 below.

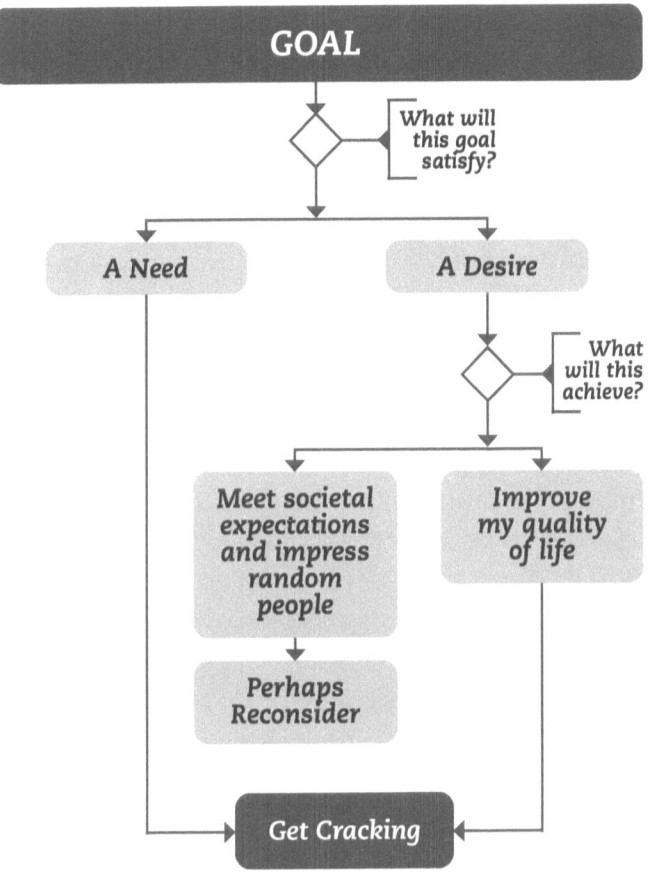

Fig. 9.1 – The motives behind our goals

I'll go back to the example about clothing, particularly expensive, branded clothing. I must reiterate a point that cannot be over-emphasized – stop trying to impress people you don't know! When you master the art of not caring about the opinions of people that carry no relevance in your life, you become mentally liberated, less stressed and, consequently, your Happiness Score goes up.

While many of us go out and buy designer label clothing purely to impress people we don't even know, there are other reasons – valid and sensible ones – for buying designer clothing. The obvious ones are quality and fit. There is a certain well-known brand of jeans that I have now taken to. They are not cheap, and for that reason I finally brought myself to buy my first pair at the grand old age of 38. I instantly fell in love with them. They fit me perfectly and they've remained in very good nick for years, maintaining their shape. The brand name itself is unimportant to me. And to be honest, its largely inconspicuous on the jeans themselves, unlike those t-shirts with logos as big and as bold as could possibly be for the world to see. These jeans fit me perfectly, and they last. Not only that, but it's one of the few brands that has dual sizing – waist *and* leg. I'm tall and slim, and my body structure has caused me endless frustrations every time I've wanted to buy a pair of trousers or jeans. Nine times out of ten, I've had to compromise on the fit. If the waist fits, then generally the leg is too short; or if the leg is the right length, the waist is too big. With this particular brand the 32 waist/ 34 leg could well have been tailor-made specifically for me. What a pleasure. And then, of course, there is the time factor. A factor whose immense importance and value goes unnoticed far too often. If I think back to previous jean-shopping escapades, I've spent at least two hours each time, going from store to store, trying on different (cheaper) brands, different sizes, different cuts etc trying to find something resembling a perfect fit. That is all a thing of the past. I know the brand, the style, and the size. And I know that they will fit me perfectly without trying them on.

Perhaps most important is the feeling I get when I look in the mirror wearing these jeans. I look good. More particularly, I look good *to myself*. I have succeeded in *impressing myself*. When you do that, you arm yourself with immense self-confidence when you leave the house, going about whatever it is that you are going about. Aim to impress yourself when you look in the mirror, rather than strangers you might walk past. When you succeed in impressing yourself, you become bullet proof. You can step out and engage with anyone you meet with 100% self-confidence. In so doing you eliminate any stress and negativity associated with negative self-image. And you increase your Happiness Score.

The principle illustrated in Fig 9.1 applies to everything you're doing. Think about buying a new car. Again, ask yourself *why?* Is it to show your neighbour, whom you despise, that you are successful? Is it to impress every stranger that pulls up next to you at the traffic lights? Or is it because a new car will improve the quality of life for you and your family? Because you're tired of your old jalopy breaking down every month, because it causes you stress, and lowers your Happiness Score. Or because you'd like to start going on more road trips – which will make you and your family happy – but your current car is not reliable enough? Go ahead and get the car (or *plan* to get the car when your finances permit) but do it for the right reasons!

When you are financially able to provide a good standard of living for yourself and your family that, in itself, should impress you. There are millions out there that cannot afford even the most basic things, and I would guess that such a situation represents the single biggest stress for any parent. You should look in the mirror every day and tell yourself that you are doing well *in your own eyes*. And when you can do that, *without* comparing yourself to those Joneses, you will have taken a giant step towards authentic happiness.

Trying to impress someone else costs *your* money, *your* time and *your* energy, yet adds nothing to *your* own happiness at the end of the day. That's just silly! Don't let that be you.

Impress yourself instead of trying to impress people who mean nothing in your life.

CHAPTER 10

THE DIFFERENT SHADES OF YOU

In a way, life is the sum of our relationships. Every waking hour is spent feeding and nurturing one relationship or another, whether directly or indirectly. But there is more to it than meets the eye.

This concept I created – *The Different Shades of You* – was born of a simple idea which, in turn, was sparked by the new normal that was forced upon us all by the Covid-19 pandemic; the new normal that gave us "work from home", "on-line schooling" and other associated catch phrases that became ways of life. In short, everyone's daily routine underwent radical, wholesale changes with little choice in the matter. Pockets of time that were previously allocated to the daily work commute were now being allocated to other activities. Children who were previously in the care of the teachers at school, suddenly had to be taken care of at home in the middle of what would ordinarily have been a day in the office for their parents.

Amid all these non-negotiable, covid-induced

adaptations, I suddenly saw things through a very different, and exceptionally clear lens. Our daily routines, and within them the various actions we take and the various pockets of time we routinely and often mindlessly allocate at various points during the day, are each geared towards a specific aspect of our lives. I coined these, *The Different Shades of You*, and there are many. *You the parent, you the spouse/partner, you the child, you the sibling, you the friend, you the physiological being, you the spiritual being, and the often unrecognised you – just you.* All these (and other) shades of ourselves make us complete beings. They give us a fulfilling life. And, importantly, each specific shade is linked to a relationship. Appendix A to this book, which is a full chapter from *The Different Shares of You*[10], will give a better understanding and appreciation of the concept.

To remain healthy, each shade of you and the relationship to which it attaches must be fed and nurtured. And for this to happen, time is paramount. If you cannot set aside ample time for a particular relationship, that relationship – that shade of you – will slowly but surely fade away and eventually die.

Like I said, there is more to relationships than meets the eye. Here is an explanatory extract from *The Different Shades of You*:[11]

> People, by nature, are gregarious beings. So, human relationships are not only natural,

they are also necessary. The Covid-induced lockdown has served, among many other things, to highlight the human need for relationships. Without relationships and the company that they bring, loneliness quickly sets in. Before you know it, loneliness becomes depression, and that road can very easily lead to suicide.

According to conventional understanding, a relationship is the connection between two or more people, and their behaviour towards each other. But I'd like to bring a couple of twists to this accepted understanding.

Firstly, each relationship is not just a connection between two people. It is more nuanced than that. When you have a relationship with someone – anyone – that other person not only connects with you but, more precisely, with a specific shade of you. Whether their expectations are justified or not, some people in your life are more demanding than others. And the natural consequence of this is that, in order to please these people, you will naturally have to favour the shade of yourself that these people connect to. Unless, of course, you change the default setting by becoming mindful of the existence and importance of all these different shades of yourself.

Secondly, the conventional understanding of relationships should be expanded to include those relationships between the different shades within us. Some shades are not involved at all in your relationships with others. Instead, the health of these shades and, in some instances, their very existence, depends entirely on the relationships they have with other shades of you. This may sound cryptic on the face of things, so we'll look at some common examples that play out in life so often.

Let's look at the shade I call *you, the physiological being*. This shade is concerned primarily with the things required for you to stay alive. Things that don't come from relationships with others. One such requirement is sleep. The rule of thumb – according to accepted science – tells us that we all need about eight hours of sleep a day. The vast majority of us know this very well, yet we still routinely sacrifice hours of sleep in the name of doing "more important things". Perhaps the most common "more important thing" is work. So, what this means in the context of the different shades of you is that *you, the employee* (which wants/needs this important work to be done) has bullied *you, the physiological being* (which needs the sleep) into relinquishing a few hours. And because of this dominance, coupled with your default setting of a lack of mindfulness, the shade *you, the physiological being* suffers silently. And, eventually, your overall health will suffer with it.

As we get older and new shades get added to our portfolio (*you the spouse* and – by far the most demanding – *you the parent*), there is obviously and unavoidably less time available to allocate to previously existing shades. It is like accounting. When one shade is credited with an extra hour, another shade must be debited with that same hour. Among the most common casualties are friendships and what I call *you, just you*. Losing certain friendships is not necessarily a bad thing. We outgrow people, and that's natural. That's life. But *you, just you*, is a different story. This is the shade that involves doing the things you like. Nothing more, nothing less. Reading books, making model aeroplanes, going for hikes on your own, sitting for a couple of hours watching your favourite sports team… whatever you enjoy doing. These activities are critical to our mental health, wellbeing, fulfilment and happiness! As we get older and garner new shades and the added responsibilities and time-demands that come with them, it is so easy for *you, just you* to fade away. And it's even easier to make excuses for it. The all too common "I don't have enough time". Don't let it happen, and don't make excuses. Make a deliberate and conscious effort to allocate enough time to nurture that shade. It is imperative to your overall fulfilment and your happiness.

What we should be coming to realise at this stage is that the relationships we *don't* have - those that we allowed to fade away – are just as important as those that we do have. They can, and do, impact our happiness just as much, but in a negative way. When we allow certain relationships and shades of ourselves to slip away, even passively and unknowingly as it can often be, whatever we may tell ourselves thereafter, there will be underlying regret. Here's another extract below from The Different Shades of You[12] that captures this aspect well:

> "This regret relates to your failure to allocate the necessary resources to certain shades at the time you could have and should have done so. But by the time you come to this realisation, the ship has already sailed. Certain relationships, and the corresponding shades they involve, have faded away so far into oblivion that they are all-but impossible to resuscitate! In many cases, you carry the heavy burden of this regret around with you for the rest of your life."

That underlying regret causes us stress. And stress, as we know, negatively impacts our Happiness Score.

Relationships come and go. But the ones that may, perhaps, illicit the most regret are those that we tried to hold on to but failed to. Or, more accurately, those that we *think* we tried to hold on to. But this act of "trying to hold on", far too often, comes in the form of substituting time for money. We refuse – whether expressly or tacitly – to give some relationships their fair share of our time, and we think it will suffice to throw more money at them instead. It doesn't work. Ever! The only relationship in which your money constitutes an acceptable substitute for your time is a superficial one. And it will not add to your happiness. At best, it will provide fleeting pleasure.

If there is one lesson to be learned from this chapter, it is this:

The active relationships we have, and those we should have but do not, directly impact our happiness.

PART IV
MONEY

FOREWORD ON MONEY

It has come to my realisation that the content in this part of the book – money – has a very high propensity to induce misunderstanding and misinterpretation. This is due, *inter alia*, to inherent prejudices as well as the way a largely capitalist society has conditioned us to think (or, more accurately, *not* think). Consequently, I would be doing disservice to both myself and the reader if I were merely to share my own views on this highly emotional and subjective topic without first laying a foundation and setting the context within which my views must be considered.

I should, perhaps, start by clarifying what this part of the book *is not*, and is *not intended* to be. It is not a wholesale discreditation of money and all that it represents and can represent. It is not an idealistic preaching against the inherent value of money in modern society. And it is certainly not a suggestion that anyone should aim for a life of stringent austerity (although there are people who choose to do this of their own accord, and for their own reasons, which is absolutely fine) in the belief that money does not, and will not, contribute positively to one's happiness and success. It is not intended to cast a shadow of cynical scepticism across *everything* that money is and has come to represent.

Money *does* have inherent worth – both at face value and in a representative capacity. To think or suggest otherwise would be nonsensical. The intention of this part of the book is to exercise and encourage *Clear Thinking*, as R.W. Jepson[13] aptly puts it. That is my overall intention in this, and all my previous books, but I believe it is most pertinent to the topic of money. The intention is to help the reader make the necessary distinction between what we see and experience for ourselves, versus what we have inferred, often unconsciously and/or through propaganda, especially in this crazy social media age.

To repeat, and to reiterate, lest the reader form a premature conclusion that this part of the book is idealistic nonsense with no practical application in real life, this is not a blanket trivialisation of the value of money and the role it plays in life. It is an exposé, of sorts, of the less savoury aspects of money that we don't, or choose not to, notice. It serves to give a more complete, and less biased view of this thing called money. This thing that so many of us subconsciously, or even consciously, worship. It serves to help rid the reader of this mindlessly and erroneously perceived omnipotence such that the positives that it *does* bring to life, with their limitations it must be said, can be seen clearly.

Here's a profound passage from Jepson[14], which is highly relevant and applicable when it comes to money, its accumulation and its value:

> "When any belief is popularly held, perhaps because it brings comfort or pleasure to its holders, every fresh circumstance is made to support and confirm it; and although many strong evidences may seem to contradict it, people either shut their eyes to them or depreciate them or get rid of them in some other way rather than sacrifice their cherished conviction."

The point of the next few chapters is to nudge readers away from popular beliefs about money that have been blindly accepted thus far; and to consider opposing evidence with some level of seriousness and open-mindedness rather closing our eyes to it or depreciating it.

CHAPTER 11

MONEY: ILLUSION AND OBSESSION

I could certainly write a whole book about money. In all likelihood, I shall do exactly that at some point, such is our ever-growing fascination as human beings by this complex creation of ours – money. But for now, we shall have to make do with a few chapters summarising, condensing and demystifying some of the most important aspects of this thing we call *money*. This thing that seemingly rules our lives, whether rightly or wrongly; whether consciously or subconsciously.

Let's start by re-visiting a passage from chapter 7, which serves to buttress the overarching point being made in the Foreword to this section of the book – Part IV.

> "Our needs must be met in order for us to have any decent quality of life, or life at all! This is the non-negotiable foundation upon which happiness is built. If these needs cannot or are not being met then, no matter how hard we may try, we will not be in a state of contentment or happiness. This is a simple fact of life. Like it or not. And yes, to address

> the elephant that has now planted itself in the room, meeting many of these needs does require money. As much as we might like to, we can't get away from the necessity of money, within limits, of course. We look at this more in Part IV."

Money is necessary. Money is not inherently evil. But money is also overrated. It is ultimately just a tool that we should use in the best possible manner, rather than becoming a mindless slave to it.

Over the course of centuries we have, somehow, been brainwashed into thinking that money itself can, and should, be a goal. Even *the* life goal for some. There are several books – best sellers at that – which are specifically focused, quite simply, on making a lot of money. And, of course, we've all heard people say "Oh, I wish I could just win the lottery." We've probably all said it ourselves at some point or, at the very least, thought it. Because, at face value, having more money would immediately solve our problems and make our lives better. And, dare I say, make us *happier*. But would it really? Of course not. This is The Trap we spoke about right at the beginning in chapter 1.

WHAT WOULD YOU DO WITH A MILLION DOLLARS?

I decided to conduct an informal survey of sorts. It resulted in a set of responses from over 100 people aged between 30 and 80 years, and from various different socio-economic, educational, geographical and ethnic backgrounds. The survey was simple. It comprised one seemingly straightforward question, which I'd like you to try and answer before you read on:

> If you won a million dollars in the lottery today, what would you do with it <u>in the next 10 days</u>?

I shall refer to this question several times during the course of this and subsequent chapters. For ease of reference, let's call it the *Million Dollar Question*.

The answers varied noticeably when it came to intricate details and specifics. But in terms of overriding principles, there were some notable constants or near constants. And on the whole they were not surprising. The most prominent constant was the intention to invest; to grow this newly acquired bounty. Every single response, bar one, expressly included the word *invest*. And that is telling in many respects. This unanimous interest in investing, together with other aspects of the responses I got, appears to confirm what I had already suspected: Money is an illusion and an obsession.

(There was one response which was simply "Vegas". Knowing the person in question, I am certain that this was in jest, and I have chosen not to include this response in my analysis.)

THE ILLUSION

I don't watch much TV. Aside from sports over the weekend, the TV I watch is confined to the movies that my children choose for us to watch together in 15–20-minute daily doses every evening before I take them to bed; and two to three nights a week watching with my wife after the children are in bed. We choose a series and watch it from start to finish – from the first to the last season. It generally takes us about six months to watch a full series, and then we move on to another one.

We recently finished the hit series *Money Heist*, which I highly recommend as much for its entertainment value as for its ability to exercise the mind in a different way. Anyone who has watched this series will have obviously picked up on the depiction of money as an illusion of sorts.

Without giving too much away, the first season revolves around the central plot of the most daring and unprecedented of bank robberies. But it is not a bank robbery as you would expect. The protagonists plan to break into the Royal Mint of Spain. There, they will not steal any money. Well, not any existing money. Rather, they will lock themselves in, and they will print new money, which is what they will then "steal". The Professor – ringleader of the gang and mastermind of the ingenious plan – is at pains to explain to the gang that they are not stealing any money belonging to the public and, for this reason, they shall become heroes in the public eye, rather than villains.

There is a now-famous scene in which The Professor delivers an emotional monologue to the captured chief investigating officer while the heist is underway:

> "You've been taught to see that there's only good and bad. But what we're doing is okay when other people do it. Is that it? In 2011 the European Central Bank made 171 billion Euros out of nothing. Just like we're doing, only larger. 185 billion in 2012. 145 billion Euros in 2013. Do you know where all that money went? To the bankers. Directly from the mint to their pockets. Did anyone say that the European Central Bank was a thief? Liquidity injections they called it. They pulled it out of nowhere, Raquel. Out of nothing.
>
> I'm making a liquidity injection, but not for the bankers. I'm doing it here, in the real economy. With this group of losers, which is what we are Raquel. To get away from it all. Don't you want to escape?"

But this series is fiction. And this scene must be designed specifically to trigger emotion and feelings of sympathy and support for the fictional characters, and to add to the overall thrill of the show. There is nothing real about it, right? Well, let's look at an excerpt from a CNN article[15] on 21 December 2011:

> "The ECB allotted €489.19 billion ($643.18 billion) in the first batch of its 3-year loan

> program – more than investors expected. The loans will go to 523 banks in the eurozone to support bank lending and liquidity, the central bank said.
>
> The ECB had announced a series of "non-standard" measures earlier this month, designed to boost liquidity for European banks struggling to secure funding in the wholesale market."

What we see here is that, although *Money Heist* is a largely fictional TV series, there are important factual elements within the fictional context. It is a fact that the European Central Bank created almost 500 billion Euros out of nothing. It is a fact that the newly created money was allocated exclusively to commercial banks as opposed to any man on the street who was suffering the effects of the recession. I would go as far as saying that most lay people to this day have no idea, really, what happened to all that newly created money; and, in any event, would not be able to make head or tail of any formal explanation offered by the banking community as it would be, probably by design, littered with technical terms and concepts which any banker would know are not understandable to the lay person.

The European Central Bank actually *did* do exactly what the fictional Professor accused it of doing. In real life! According to this CNN article, the injection went to commercial banks, to "support lending and liquidity". It's a fair assumption that the bulk of the injection was then lent out by those banks to their clients. Interest charges aside, it is all but common knowledge that bank loans and facilities attract an establishment fee ranging between 1% and 2.5% of the amount lent and borrowed. That is a fee that is paid by the borrower for the privilege of being given a bank loan. Doing some simple arithmetic, that equates to between 4.9 billion and 12.3 billion Euros "earned" by commercial banks on establishment fees alone. Billions of dollars in their pockets for merely onward-lending money that was newly created by the central bank. What do we call that?

Let me share another story that will undoubtedly sound like made-for-TV fiction – but is quite the opposite. It is as real as things can get, and I know because I lived through it. It was 2019 in Zimbabwe, but it was the culmination of events dating back more than ten years. By the end of 2008 the Zimbabwean economy had completely and utterly crumbled. Grocery store shelves were empty, and those stores that were stocked with your non-basic goods were increasing their prices three to four times per day. The local currency was literally worthless. From 2008 to 2009, the currency was redenominated twice, with a cumulative total of twenty-three zeros being removed. That means that a Zimbabwe Dollar amount of 1.00 in early 2009 was actually 100,000,000,000,000,000,000,000 pre-2008 (one hundred sextillion). The exchange rate, *after* the removal of those 23 zeros was

US$1: ZW$ 35,000,000,000,000,000 (35 quadrillion). Inflation was 231,000,000%.[16] Disaster and chaos do not even begin to describe the state of affairs!

Soon after the third currency re-denomination in early 2009 the Zimbabwe dollar, in all its iterations, was abolished altogether and the United States Dollar became the official currency of the country. There was, finally, some financial order and stability in the land. This all worked very well for several years. Salaries were denominated and paid in US$, as were the prices of goods and services. US$ cash was readily available in ATM machines. Life was, in a word, normal.

Normalcy would not last too long. In Zimbabwe, everyone is well-conditioned to expect the next wave of chaos and calamity at very short notice and, indeed, that next wave was upon us by 2014. It was triggered by the introduction by the Zimbabwe Central Bank of a new monetary form called the "bond coin". The rationale, we were told, was that there was no circulation of United States coins in the country (which was true), and this had created problems for merchants who needed to give change to their cash customers (which was also true). The solution was for the Central Bank to mint its own coins which, we were told, would carry the same value as the United States Dollar. So a 50 cent Zimbabwe bond coin carried equivalent value to 50 United States cents. Very soon, there was a $1 Zimbabwe bond coin which, similarly, was said to carry the same value as one United States Dollar. Now, the economy was flooded with $1 United States Dollar bills, so the introduction of a $1 Zimbabwe Bond Coin (followed by $2 and $5 bills) naturally created not only confusion, but scepticism and panic. What we now had, which was clear for all to see, was two *de facto* currencies – the United States Dollar; and the Zimbabwe Bond coin/note which was unconvincingly masquerading as a United States Dollar!

The people and the markets quickly picked up this glaring distinction. In a short space of time it became very difficult to withdraw cash in the form of genuine United States dollars. Simultaneously, an unofficial dual pricing system emerged. Payments using United States Dollars cash attracted one price. Payments using other methods – bank card, bank transfer or Real Time Gross Settlement (RTGS) – attracted a different price. The latter was slightly higher than the former, maybe by about 5%. If an item was priced at US$1.00 that was the price you would pay in United States dollars cash. But you would pay US$1.05 using one of the other methods. Now, let's keep in mind that bank accounts had not changed. At least not officially. The balance a person had in their bank was a United States dollar balance. When you paid using your bank card or via bank transfer, you were – officially speaking – paying United States dollars. But that was not the practical reality.

This unofficial exchange rate gradually grew,

month on month from the 1.00: 1.05 at which it started. By the latter part of 2018 the unofficial rate had reached 1:2, and by early February 2019, it was 1:4. To be sure, that meant that in early February, one United States dollar in cash was worth four United States dollars trapped in your bank account. Crazy, right?

The best (or worst) lay ahead. On 22 February 2019, Statutory Instrument 33 of 2019 was gazetted. In a nutshell, it had a dual effect: Firstly, it created a new currency. Just to add to the ridiculousness of the story, the new currency was named the RTGS dollar! Secondly, it had the effect of magically transforming all amounts held in banks, investment houses, pension funds as well as all debts from Unites States dollars to this new currency – the RTGS dollar. Literally overnight. What this meant was that if you had US$1,000 in your bank account on 21 February 2019, you then had RTGS$1,000 in your bank account on 22 February 2019.

The RTGS dollar was given a value. One United States dollar was officially equivalent to 2.5 RTGS dollars. As I've already mentioned, however, the unofficial rate that prevailed in reality was already 1:4. So what this meant was that all your savings, investments and debts receivable suddenly carried a quarter of the value you might have thought they did 24 hours earlier. The flipside was that if owed somebody money your indebtedness was reduced to a quarter of what it previously was. I wrote an article for the Commonwealth Lawyers Association entitled *How the Law turned Debtors into Kings*. You can find it in the appendices.

So what happened? For five years, up to 21 February 2019, the express message from the Zimbabwe Central Bank and each person's own respective Commercial Bank was that the balances in our accounts were United States Dollars. What happened to those United States Dollars that, overnight, were replaced by a different currency? Where did the United States dollars go? Were they there at all or was it an illusion that we were living for five years?

"We will be their heroes" said the Professor in *Money Heist*. But, again, it's a fictional series, right? Well, let's consider this headline from the very much non-fictional BBC News:

- **Lebanon man hailed hero for holding Beirut bank hostage over savings.**[17]

Did this man get his idea from *Money Heist*? Who knows, and quite frankly, who cares? There are far more important questions that we should be asking, which we shall get to shortly. In summary, this man had savings to the value of US$210,000 and wanted to withdraw $5,500 to pay hospital bills, and the bank refused. The bank refused to give him a mere 2.6% of *his own* money that they were "keeping safely" for him. I have lived through similarly trying economic times where it was near to impossible to get cash out of the bank. And, at the same time, you would have service providers like medical practitioners demanding cash because they knew that bank transfers carried significantly less value. At the end of a six-hour saga, which began with the man entering the bank with a rifle and pouring petrol in the banking hall, he was allowed to leave with $35,000.

The questions that come to my mind are: Where was the $210,000 that this man "had" in the bank? If it wasn't there, why hadn't the bank said so instead of issuing statements saying that it *was* there? Most importantly, did that $210,000 ever exist or was it always an illusion?

While every respondent to my million-dollar question bar one specifically mentioned investment, over 90% had no idea where, when or how they would go about this intended investment. They were content to park their winnings in the bank for the first 10 days and beyond until they had some concrete plan on how to invest. On how to turn this money into more money. What we see here is the lack of any intention to actually *use* that money, whether to acquire anything or to tangibly change anything in one's life in the immediate term, whether today, tomorrow or in ten days' time. Life continues just as it was yesterday, only with an extra million dollars now sitting in your bank account. There, *somewhere*, floating around these clever creations called the banking and monetary systems.

This monetary system, and what is in it, can so often be an illusion. An illusion of what you have. And, consequently, an illusion that everything is good in life, specifically because of that which you "have". But if you think about it, that money that is tucked away in the bank is really just a sequence of digits on the e-statement you pull up on your banking app every now and again. If you were to walk into the bank, whether you are in troubled Lebanon, Zimbabwe or anywhere else, and ask to physically withdraw those million dollars in cold, hard cash (*actual* as opposed to *illusory* money), you would not be able to. You would be given all sorts of reasons, including a plethora of anti-money laundering regulations, liquidity ratios and others. But you would not get your cash – "your" cash – because they do not have it. And you certainly wouldn't get it for an extended period of time, possibly ever. Rather than actual, physical money, you would have to (and we all generally do) make do with what the bank tells you that you "have"; and with the things you are able to acquire with it by way of transactions that "move money" somewhere in cyberspace. But the money itself – the actual cold, hard cash – well ... no! You can't have it. Well not much of it anyway.

If you still beg to differ, let's take a look at some financial headlines:

- **There's an $80 trillion 'blind spot' in the financial system that could spell trouble for**

markets as debts held off-balance sheet grow at a rapid pace.
Business Insider – 7 December 2022[18]

- **Visualizing $65 Trillion in Hidden Dollar Debt (by non- U.S. Banks and shadow banks.)**
  Visual Capitalist – 8 January 2023[19]

- **'It'll wipe out every dollar in the world' - new crash fears as $80trillion 'goes missing'.**
  The Express UK – 7 December 2022[20]

These headlines are mind-boggling in every sense. What is a person supposed to think when they read these headlines and stories? What is really going on? Does anyone really know? We can't really answer any of those questions. And the inability of anyone to properly answer these questions provides an answer to a different question – is the concept of money largely illusory? It looks very much that way.

Let's go back to the responses to my Million-Dollar Question, in particular the investment stage. After all, it's what everyone plans to do at some point after the initial 10 days. Many of the assets that you may invest in carry an even bigger illusory element than your bank balance. Imagine investing in a particular stock and then it somehow loses 20% of its value overnight. And it can be triggered by something as simple as one person's social media post. Well, don't imagine.

Not only can it happen, but it has happened.[21] 20% equates to a whopping $200,000 of your new million that has literally disappeared into thin air. Overnight! Or was it always just thin air? Either way, it does sound very much like an illusion.

Here's another brilliantly baffling headline from Bloomberg:

- **Elon Musk becomes the first person ever to lose $200 billion.**[22]

What does this really mean? Where has that $200 billion gone? The answer is that it hasn't gone anywhere because it never really existed to start with. The things that existed were investment instruments (another clever creation that facilitates further illusory creation, and loss, of money) in the form of stocks, bonds, options and others. Those instruments still exist. It's just that their value fluctuates day to day, hour to hour. But who exactly decides when and how they fluctuate? Well, we don't really know, do we? It's part of the illusion.

While we're at it, let's spare a thought for Bernie Madoff's investors. Month upon month, year upon year, for almost two decades they received monthly trading statements showing balances collectively worth over US$60 billion. $60 billion that didn't exist! Only years later the house of cards came tumbling down and Madoff's fraudulent scheme was exposed.[23] Those monthly investment statements really were an illusion in every sense of the word.

There were signs that something wasn't right with Madoff's investments. And some investors saw the signs, and even reduced their investments but didn't withdraw them completely. In his book *Talking to Strangers* Malcolm Gladwell[24] talks about some of the intricacies of Madoff's Ponzi scheme from the perspective of investors:

> "In November 2003, Nat Simons, a portfolio manager for the Long Island based hedge fund Renaissance Technologies, wrote a worried email to several of his colleagues …
>
> … The next day Henry Laufer, one of the firm's senior executives, wrote back. He agreed. Renaissance, he added, had 'independent evidence' that something was amiss with Madoff. Then Renaissance's risk manager, Broder – the person responsible for making sure the fund didn't put its money anywhere dangerous – weighed in with a long, detailed analysis of the trading strategy that Madoff claimed to be using. 'None of it seems to add up', he concluded …
>
> Did Renaissance sell off its stake in Madoff? Not quite. They cut their stake in half."

Gladwell's explanation for this absurd behaviour lies in what he calls "default to truth", which essentially explains the way we are almost invariably inclined to see things only in a certain way. A way that doesn't deviate much from the easiest mental path. A way that allows us to hold on to beliefs so deeply set in our psyche through years and years of being conditioned, often unknowingly. To think in any other way would quite simply be too much like mental hard work. We try our best to make the story that we hear a credible story, which in turn becomes a true story in our minds.

But I believe there is more to it than that. There must be, for we're not talking about average people believing random stories. We're talking about highly trained and highly experienced investment and risk management professionals who chose to go against everything they had learned, and all evidence they had accumulated, to make billion-dollar investments. That is not merely defaulting to truth. It is untold greed and the promise of unrealistically high returns that got the better of them and their decision-making skills; and made them buy into what was, clearly, an illusion of money. Money in the form of returns that, deep down, they knew didn't and couldn't really exist.

But I'm not a financial advisor, and this is not – nor is it intended to be – investment (or non-investment) advice. Rather, it's something to trigger a thought process that deviates from that which has been mindlessly accepted as the norm when it comes to money.

Let me not delve any deeper into the intricacies of monetary systems, stock markets, Ponzi schemes and the illusory aspects of money. More importantly, let me not dampen the spirits of all the aspiring (or actual) millionaire readers any further. That is not the point of this book. Let's put aside the scepticism, cynicism and the portrayal of money as an illusion, and proceed on the assumption that money is money as we are led to believe.

THE MINDLESS OBSESSION

It was a Friday evening in 2000 – my freshman year at university in Johannesburg. We were only a few weeks into the academic year and about five of us newbies, all in the same hall of residence, had become pretty close. There we were, sitting in one of the guys' dormitory room, doing what we so often did – drinking beer, listening to hip-hop music and playing chess (Yes, I know, we were not your stereotypical chess players) as we considered our bigger plans for the night ahead.

As the hours passed, it became clear that the will and the energy to go out and have a night on the town had all but evaporated. But we had a problem. We were almost out of beer! Fortunately, we had a guest on this occasion. One of our group had invited someone from his faculty to join us. Unlike the rest of us, our guest had a car and a working knowledge of Johannesburg. What was to follow is the stuff of legends!

The lack of energy in the room coupled with the waning beer supplies sparked our guest into a series of declarations. And so he began…

"Listen guys, I'm going to get another case of beer. Actually no – I'm going to get another three cases of beer! And when I bring them back, we're going to drink and drink and drink as much as we can! And after that, do you know what we'll do?" We looked at each other, all wondering what we could possibly do after drinking as much beer as we could, apart from perhaps passing out. Before anyone could offer a suggestion, our guest shared the correct answer – "We will drink some more!"

There is a point to that little story, aside from me recalling my youth and the nostalgic feelings that come with it. The point is that this is precisely how we think about money. We want more and more and more of it; and after that … we want more still when, objectively speaking, it neither makes any sense nor makes any difference to our lives. To close off the story, for those with curious minds like mine, our guest didn't end up going to get any more beer, and the night petered out very tamely.

One particular respondent answered my Million Dollar Question with such simplicity, clarity and conviction, that it must be shared verbatim (incidentally this was the solitary response that didn't expressly include the word "invest"):

> "I would buy real estate to generate rentals. And I would use the rentals to buy more real estate. Small, medium, big. Just buy!"

Like most of the responses, this one showed a distinct absence of any intention to actually *use* (as opposed to *invest*) the winnings. But what really jumped out at me from this response was the absence of any intention to later use the return on the investment. It's all about accumulating more and more; and re-investing and re-investing. But for what, really?

The universal default setting "to invest" represents strong evidence of the way we have been brainwashed into believing that the acquisition of money can be and should be a goal in itself. We have every single respondent wanting this new and substantial sum of money to become a more substantial sum. And after that? More again! The actual use of that money appears to be unimportant. Just as long as the amount is growing, wherever it is. I'm sorry... it just doesn't seem to make sense to use a million dollars to generate more and more money when, if we're being honest, you don't actually know what to do with the first million. What then would you do with the second, and third? It is accumulating more money for the sake, purely, of accumulating more money. What is the point of it all? And at what cost?

MONEY BUYS PLEASURE (AND IT'S NOT THAT IMPORTANT)

Not a single survey response made mention of any shopping spree whatsoever, with less than 5% of the respondents saying they would go on holiday to celebrate. I guess rushing off to buy an expensive performance car when you win the lottery is just a cliché after all.

This portrays, almost universally, what appears to be tacit and subconscious acknowledgement and acceptance of one of the cornerstones of this book, which was unpacked in detail in chapter 5 – the distinction between happiness and pleasure. A critical distinction which, unfortunately, becomes blurred when the conscious mind takes over.

It is this tacit acknowledgement of the distinction that explains the conspicuous absence of indulgent spending. Because that would amount to pleasure and, somewhere deep down below the surface of our brainwashed conscious minds, we all know that mere pleasure – no matter how expensive – is not really what we want out of life in the grander scheme of things. We realise that is not happiness!

Despite the nonsensical obsession in the conscious mind with trying to generate more and more money without really knowing what we ultimately want to do with it, I am convinced there is a subconscious understanding that there must be something more worthwhile that we *could* do with this new money that would impact our happiness, as opposed to our desires for fleeting pleasure. And while we try to figure out what that "something more worthwhile" is, we might as well invest the money. So, in trying to make sense of this default setting to invest, I have come up with the rationale that I believe applies to the bulk of people who come into a large sum of money and choose to invest it. "Invest" is only the first part. The rest of the answer is embedded somewhere in the thought process, perhaps the subconscious, struggling to find its way out verbally. If it could, it would sound something like this:

> "I will invest it rather than waste it on unnecessary and superficial pleasures, and let it grow while I figure out how I can use it to make my life meaningfully better. And happier!"

The truth is this: Beyond meeting our daily needs with a certain level of comfort (as opposed to extravagance), money has little tangible value in the quest for happiness. Equally importantly, which we unpack in the next chapters:

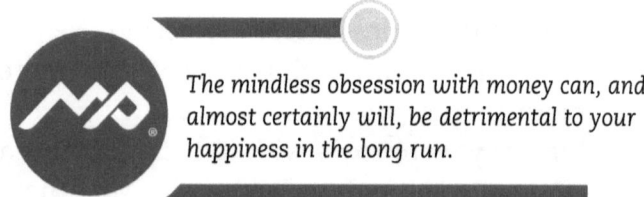

The mindless obsession with money can, and almost certainly will, be detrimental to your happiness in the long run.

CHAPTER 12

MORE MONEY, MORE PROBLEMS

This, of course, is not a hard and fast rule. It is not even a rule at all. It is a warning that, unfortunately, many never take heed of. What I would like the reader to take away from this chapter is that while we mindlessly go about chasing more and more money, on the blind assumption that it represents the answer or solution to all our problems, the reality is that more money *can*, and often *does*, lead to more problems. And I will explain and illustrate exactly how.

The more money you have, the better the lifestyle you can afford. This is obvious, and there is nothing wrong with improving your lifestyle. But let's take a step forward. The better the lifestyle you can afford, the *even better* lifestyle you begin to crave. As the saying goes, the more you earn, the more you spend. While obviously not universally true, it is a common phenomenon. Some would argue that it is embedded in human nature.

Money and the lifestyle it buys, together, create a sense of power and status. If we go back to Maslow's hierarchy, we can clearly see that the desire for status is what is being met. The power and status are like drugs that feed the ego, and they can very easily and very quickly become addictive. And so, you keep chasing more money, you keep upgrading your lifestyle, as you crave the compliments and even the envy of your "friends". But what this now means is that the bulk of your time and energy must, necessarily, be spent chasing more money and more financial success. You have created an image that must now be upheld. You have set a high bar for yourself, and you're now obliged to maintain it at the very least, if not raise it. This, as we now know, is the Trap. But what happens to the other aspects of your life? Your marriage, your children, your parents, your *real* friends who are not impressed by your financial success but, rather, disappointed at the jerk you've become. What happens to your health and your hobbies?

Problems will inevitably begin to surface in those aspects of your life – and those *Different Shades of You*. But, as I highlighted in the preface, when you're caught in the Trap, you are firmly of the belief – the mistaken belief, of course – that when you reach financial success, everything else automatically falls into place. The second aspect of the Trap is that when non-monetary aspects of your life do *not* magically fall into place as you assumed they would, the default "solution" is to throw money at them. Because you can!

So, you lavish your spouse and children with gifts that increase in price and frequency. You do the same with your parents. You buy that expensive piece of home-gym equipment, telling yourself that it will solve your physical fitness shortcomings. But the money you're throwing at all these aspects of your life – these different shades of you – is not solving any problems. You find your spouse beginning to look for affection elsewhere. In fact, he/she is using the money that you throw at them to make themselves look more attractive and more "eligible" to suitors; you find your children looking for ways of getting your attention, rather than your money. This can result in drug abuse and other undesirable outcomes. The money serves not to make your child happy but, rather, makes all sorts of pleasures – including harmful ones – easily accessible to them. Your real friends are not impressed by your money and your new attitude, and those once-meaningful relationships fade away. Suddenly the money you thought would solve your problems, has actually exacerbated them. What is needed to solve those problems is very simple. It is your time. But, because you're caught in the Trap, you find yourself compelled to spend whatever time you can on making more money, to buy more expensive things and paint the picture of success. There is simply no time for the other aspects of your life. But there is money!

Ant that's the thing about time. It's a great

equaliser. As I point out in *The Different Shades of You:*[25]

> Money is relative. There is no equality in money. A dollar is not just a dollar. For, if a millionaire donates $1 000 to charity, he has donated 0.1% of his fortune. If Average Joe, with a net worth of $20 000, donates an "equivalent" amount of $1 000, it equates to a pretty substantial 5% of his entire worth. Perhaps, to the beneficiary, a dollar is just a dollar, but to the person parting with that dollar, it is quite the opposite. And it is the latter that is more important, because everyone has a responsibility to find the right balance in the way they allocate and part with their own resources.
>
> Time, however, is the one constant in life. In everybody's life! No matter who you are and what you do, you only have 24 hours per day. So, when you give someone an hour of your time, you give them 4% of your day, and that 4% remains constant regardless of your fame and fortune, or status in society. Whether you're a beggar or a billionaire, an hour is an hour.

Life, in essence, consists of several relationships, including the relationship every person has with themselves. I go into detail in *The Different Shades of You* about how every relationship needs to be nurtured, otherwise it begins to crumble and eventually dies. The nourishment every relationship needs comes in the form of two essential resources – time and money. Every relationship needs both, though the proportion will differ depending on the nature of each individual relationship. In a nutshell, the moment you try to substitute necessary time with money, the relationship(s) will begin to develop problems. And it is only as people get more money that they gain the capacity to make that substitution. More money, more problems.

This phenomenon – "more money, more problems" – rings further true for entrepreneurs and business owners. I once had a CEO who, quite impressively, grew his business from one retail store to over 15. As a businessman he was, undoubtedly, very successful. But he once told me straight that the more money there is, the more money there is for the staff to steal. He was obsessed with staff stealing. While he could easily have been correct, is this not merely another problem created by more money? Who really wants to spend their life worrying about their staff stealing, instead of truly unwinding and enjoying the fruits of their labour? Aside from that, there were several occasions when he was on family holidays thousands of miles away yet was still bashing out emails. After one of his trips, I asked him why he was not doing what people are supposed to do when they're on holiday instead of sitting in front of his computer. His answer was simple ... "I can't afford not to." I didn't take it any further. But I immediately asked myself what the point of going on holiday was when you're sitting in front of your computer for large chunks of your day… every day. I was still in my twenties back then, and quite naïve in the business sense. Now, with almost 15 years' experience in the corporate world, I totally get it… in a way. As the founder of a business, it is like your baby. Quite literally. You feel that you can't leave it alone for too long. You must take care of it, nurture it, watch it grow. You can't just take a break from it for a month. I certainly get that. But at what cost? At the expense of time spent with your real, human baby! Is it worth it?

But there is another side to the coin, as there always is. And, in my opinion, it is the more important side of the coin. Now, as a husband and a father of the two biggest blessings God and life could ever have given me, I see things differently. Very differently. If I'm on a family holiday, then that must be my primary focus. I should not be doing any work, because my family deserves more of me. And I deserve more of myself. I deserve to unwind, turn off and, quite frankly, not give a sh!t about what is going on or not going on in the office. I'm on holiday! Yes, I'm not a business owner or founder, so I could never fully appreciate what it's like to be in those shoes. But regardless, what does this mean in the grander scheme of life, when you can't truly unwind and relax on a beach somewhere for a couple of weeks because you "can't afford not to keep working"?

Ever. What kind of life is that? Is it a successful one? More pertinently, is it a happy one?

Incidentally, that CEO went through a messy divorce, and the business empire simultaneously crumbled. It should perhaps be emphasized that this is not what happens to every person, every time. It is, rather, a demonstration of what can happen.

It is important is to acknowledge the real dangers that you open yourself up to when your focus is purely on financial success.

CHAPTER 13

WOULD YOU QUIT YOUR JOB?

Imagine this scenario: You are unexpectedly approached by your employer, who presents you with two options.

- Option 1, which is simply that nothing changes; or
- Option 2, which entails the employer paying you 15 years' salary in advance, and you no longer do any work for them – neither from the office nor in the *en vogue* work-from-home realm. No work at all. That is 180 monthly pay cheques, all paid right now. Somewhere in the small print, however, it is stipulated that although you're being paid in advance, you remain contracted to that particular employer for the period of the advance payment. This means that you are prohibited from working for anyone else for the next 15 years.

_{'I shall continue to refer to these as simply Option 1 and Option 2 in this chapter and those to follow.}

Option 1 allows you to keep climbing the corporate ladder if that's your goal; or to plod along as you look for something newer and better (whatever "better" might mean to you); or to float along doing as little as possible, firmly entrenched in your comfort zone with the security of a decent pay cheque every month, all the way to retirement; or whatever it is that you find appealing about the world of formal employment. Option 2, however, sounds like a far more attractive proposition to the average person, right?

I presented this hypothetical situation to a number of the respondents to my Million Dollar Question. The answer was unanimously and, in hindsight, somewhat unsurprisingly in favour of Option 2. The looks on these people's faces told two stories. Firstly, that this was really a no-brainer of a question; and, secondly, the facial expressions very swiftly began to portray the most pleasurable thoughts and images of all the wonderful ways in which one could fill their days without the immensely burdensome mental weight of this thing called a job. That load that is ever-present – whether above or lurking just below the surface. These faces became windows to the mental machinery in overdrive. The picture of contemplation. Happy contemplation. Envisaging the old hobbies they could resuscitate and the new ones that they might like to try before old age takes its inevitable and unavoidable grip on life. All the exotic and alluring destinations they'd love to visit under this new set of circumstances. The list goes on, the images become more vivid, and the thoughts become more elaborate and enticing. I imagine that you, the reader, are finding your own mind drifting in that most desirable direction, just as I am as I write about it.

Or what about just doing the small but certainly not unimportant things that your work-induced time constraints don't allow you to. Visit your ageing parents more. And your grandparents if you're fortunate to still have them. While you're at it, you can be mentally present at family lunches every Sunday instead of sitting in silent misery with the impending Monday morning stresses weighing heavily on your mind and, unknowingly, on your face. Go and pick your children up from school when they finish early instead of letting them wait in aftercare until your workday is done. And then play with them in the afternoon. Talk to them about their school day and about life in general. Little people have their problems as well. Spend more time exercising and cooking healthy meals.

I must confess, the unanimity of the attraction of Option 2 took me by surprise at first. Firstly, because these very respondents had been distinctly averse to quitting their jobs in the wake of winning a million dollars in the lottery; and secondly, by my unrelated reasoning, the 15-year work prohibition imposed by Option 2 appears excessively restrictive. As a contingency plan in anticipation of this objection being raised, I had formulated a modified, follow up version of Option 2 which turned out to be completely unnecessary and unused, but here it is anyway: You would be prohibited from working for *anyone else* for the next 15 years, but you *would* be permitted to, should you find yourself so-inclined or even compelled, to work on and in a business you start yourself. This presents even more exciting prospects (in my mind anyway) which I shall share, despite the fact it didn't come up in my discussions. I want you, the reader, to re-think the concept of what "work" does and should entail. The options are, literally, endless. I imagine that under this set of circumstances the thought-process could look something like this:

> Could any hobbies, perhaps, be turned into a small business, since that is the only work I could possibly do if I wanted to? Maybe I could pursue my passion for poetry reading and writing and start publishing my works. Possibly a small catering business. I do love cooking after all, and I always get such compliments on my cuisine. I could get into much better shape by putting in the longer gym sessions I always wished I could but couldn't find the time for. While I'm at it, I could do the personal trainer certification course I always wanted to, and then turn that into my small business. Maybe I could be a travel blogger, sharing my experiences of all the destinations that I'll be visiting anyway. Or maybe, just maybe, I could go big. I often think back with mixed emotion – fond

memories peppered with regret – to my youth when I was something of a teen golf prodigy before college, marriage, children and my job took over. I could dust off those golf clubs. Hell, I could buy new, top of the range clubs with part of my 180 pay cheques, and work towards making the Senior PGA Tour! Why the hell not?

Whether with or without an option to work on a business you start for yourself, all things considered, it's fair to say that Option 2 would be a largely positive and most welcome development in the lives of most formally employed adults. I would go to the extent of saying that, except for those in a vocational or life-purpose related occupation, Option 2 is an appealing proposition to *all* working adults. There are many reasons for the universal appeal. Some of them are obvious and have been mentioned, but there is one less obvious but no less material than any other. It is the fact that Option 2 is not, technically, quitting one's job. It is, therefore, an option that requires little mental work in the way of decision making. In short, it is an easy choice to make.

Now, let's park those wishful and wonderful thoughts for a moment, and go back to chapter 11, and the Million Dollar Question.

There was another most interesting, yet quite unanticipated constant that presented itself. I was, and remain, astounded by it. It was this sheer bewilderment that led me to this spinoff question. Astonishingly, not a single respondent spoke about quitting their job if they won a million dollars. In some instances I took it upon myself to explicitly ask this as a follow-up to the primary survey question. 100% of the responses were negative. One respondent immediately and without hesitation, went on to add "but if it was ten million, I *would* quit my job". This is a person who had just confessed that he had no idea what he would do with *one* million dollars yet, somehow, he had instantaneously formed a conclusion that the million dollars – the one he doesn't know what to do with – is not enough!? And then, barely pausing for breath, let alone any thought, he arrived at a further conclusion that the figure of 10 million *is* "enough". Enough for what, one might (and should) wonder? Enough perhaps to make a person ten times more clueless as to what they might do with it? In short, the unanimous position was that a million dollars is deemed insufficient to quit your job. Quite dumbfounding to say the least. If this is not proof of a mindless obsession, then I don't know what is. But let's dig deeper still.

Aside from a million dollars not being enough, some insisted that they like their job. Most of these are people known to me on a very personal level. These are people whom I've witnessed first-hand routinely cringing and complaining at the prospect of returning to their "beloved" jobs after each weekend, which is said to go by far too quickly. This appears to be a global uniformity. I was recently speaking to someone from Ireland, and he shared an amusing little story of how, in his corner of the world, this very feeling came to be known as "Glenroe Fever". *Glenroe* was the name of an Irish TV series that aired every Sunday evening. As it aired, so the story goes, the theme music triggered that all too familiar, sinking, stomach-turning feeling of the end of the weekend and the imminent and dreaded return to work the following day. We all know the feeling.

These people, who claim to like their jobs, are the same people who habitually grumble, either to themselves or to whomever will listen, about the fact that they routinely have to bring their work home because of the unfair, unrealistic and simply unmanageable workloads and deadlines. But they tell themselves, and others, that they like their jobs. I've been there, so I know exactly what it's like. Thankfully I've seen the light!

How does this reconcile with the Gallup Survey which found that 85% of the estimated one billion full time employees globally "hate their job and especially their boss". The short answer is that the two simply do not reconcile with each other. Could it just be a rationalisation to say, "I like my job"? Could it be a tacit acknowledgement that the proposition on the table is merely hypothetical, so there is nothing to be gained by saying "I hate my job and I would quit in an instant."? If anything, there is something to lose.

In the minds of many people, admitting that they hate a certain aspect of their lives – in this case their job – portrays a picture of weakness and, worse, failure. It highlights a very dull reality that must be lived through. Does it perhaps serve as a coping mechanism for the continued travails of that very job, that we know we must continue to face tomorrow after this superficially gratifying but sadly theoretical discussion is behind us? I think that a lot of people *do* like *certain aspects* of their jobs, and they choose – whether consciously or subconsciously; whether rightly or wrongly – to focus on those aspects that they like rather than those they do not, rather than focusing on the job as a whole.

Let's get back to the Gallup survey. A simple application of its findings tells us that the majority (perhaps not exactly 85%, but almost certainly a majority nonetheless) of my respondents hate or at least dislike their jobs. But even with a sudden (hypothetical) windfall of a million dollars they will not quit. This is what they tell themselves anyway. They will continue to go through the misery and the stress that their job and their boss dish out daily, all in exchange not just for money (because they now have a million dollars), but for *more* money, when they don't even know what to do with the substantial amount of money they already have. No consideration is paid to the daily cost being paid for that extra money – the time, the relationships, the dreams and, most importantly the happiness. The cost of that paycheque has been rendered completely unnecessary by a new million dollars, but people are still willing – in their minds at least – to pay the cost of that pay cheque, which takes the form of their happiness, every day, every week, every month. Like I said, dumbfounding!

For you and me, this is all hypothetical. But this is the reality for many corporate executives out there. They have earned so much money over the years that they could happily retire at 50 or earlier. But they don't. They keep chasing more money, they keep putting up with the stresses of the corporate world (and these stresses are significant), and they keep paying the cost in the form of their time and their relationships.

What is also quite fascinating is the way this thought of quitting your job just because you won a million dollars is, somehow, riddled with negativity. It is almost shameful, dishonourable and shallow; while the thought of your employer paying you 15 years' salary in advance to do nothing is appealing and wholly positive. You see, in case you hadn't already noticed, these two situations are really one and the same. They both leave you with a million dollars (or close enough) and no job to go to. I shall demonstrate below for those who are not convinced.

Table 13.1 below tabulates some data from the Bureau of Labor Statistics, in particular average earnings as at March 2023[26]. I have used average annual earnings in the United States given that all monetary reference thus far has been to United States dollars; and, perhaps more importantly, it allows for a meaningful comparison with what I call "the Magic Number" which I shall get to shortly.

Average weekly earnings	Average annual earnings	15 years' earnings
1,141.39	59,352.28	890,284.20

Table 13.1 – United States Average Earnings

For the average person, 15 years' salary is actually slightly less than a million dollars. Yet we positively and pleasurably entertain Option 2; while we scoff at the idea of quitting our jobs with a bigger amount of a million dollars from the lottery. Why does it make a difference whether you receive a million dollars from the lottery and stop working; or a million dollars from your employer and stop working?

As we remember, there was a unanimous intention to invest most or all of a newly won million dollars. Average return on investment for stocks is over 10% per annum, and real estate between 8 and 10% per annum.[27] Looking at hedge fund investments, which carry lower risk than stocks, Forbes reported in 2022[28] the average return is 7.2%, with the average among the top 50 funds in the United States sitting at 15.5%. If we take the low end of the spectrum – 7.2% – we get the "worst case scenario" as it were. This worst-case scenario still translates to an annual return of $72,000, which is significantly more than the average annual earning.

What this means in simplified terms is that, on average, you will earn more from investing a million dollars than you will earn from your job (that 85% of employed people hate). And, importantly, this is *without* touching the million dollars itself.

Of course there are people who have salaries that are higher (and lower) than that captured in table 13.1. And, of course, there are readers who live and work outside the United States. In the grander scheme of things, however, I put it to you that these variables are largely irrelevant in the context of an argument that a million dollars is "not enough". Such an argument, in short, is nonsensical. But it gets worse.

In his fascinating book *Thinking, Fast and Slow* Daniel Kahneman[29] explores what he describes as *the sense of well-being that people experience as they live their lives*. This looks very much like a(nother) definition of happiness. As he investigates, Kahneman considers the role of money in the level of wellbeing experienced by people as they go about their lives, making reference to the analysis of over 450,000 responses from a

Gallup-Healthways Well-being Index survey. His conclusions are most interesting:

> "The satiation level beyond which experienced well-being no longer increases was a household income of $75,000 in high-cost areas which could be less in areas where the cost of living is lower. The average increase of experienced well-being associated with incomes beyond that level is precisely zero."

What this is saying, with evidence to support it, is that beyond an amount of $75,000 per household per annum, money has no impact whatsoever on one's sense of well-being as you live your life. And, by simplified extension, it has no effect on one's happiness. This would appear to confirm my opinion from chapter 7 that beyond meeting one's needs, with a certain level of comfort of course, money has little or no impact on one's happiness. I'm going to call this $75,000 per annum per household "the Magic Number". Maybe, just maybe, the Magic Number represents a plausible (and surprisingly low) answer to one of humankind's age-old questions: *How much is enough?* Some food for thought, perhaps, for those who opined that an amount of one million dollars is "not enough to quit my job".

Going by Kahneman's findings, read in the context of the very conservative return on investment of 7.2% we looked at earlier, the investment of a million dollars will give you just shy of the Magic Number! It is, in fact, enough for you to quit your job. It allows you to live a comfortable life with a monthly income (through return on investment) that is just shy of the Magic Number, thus maximising your experienced well-being occasioned by money; whilst simultaneously giving you all the time in the world to do what you choose to do. And, for good measure, there's a bonus – your million dollars remains untouched for that notorious, eternally-looming but seldom arriving "rainy day". More money will undoubtedly give you ready access to more luxuries and more pleasures, but evidence suggests it will not make you any happier. Not one bit!

Let me take a short digression for a moment, one that I feel is somewhat necessary in this day and age. The Magic Number puts the concept of a billion dollars and this nouveau-trendy creature called the billionaire into perspective. Simple arithmetic tells us that a billion dollars is equivalent to over 13,000 years (for the avoidance of doubt, that is thirteen thousand years) of earning \$75,000 per year. That is mind blowing. Yet there are people who obsess about being billionaires; and billionaires who are fixated upon the next billion, and the next billions after that. Perhaps they think they will live 13,000 years to enjoy that billion; and then another 13,000 years after that?

Why then are people so averse to the idea of quitting their jobs? People who are visibly stressed, stretched and strained by their jobs on a weekly, if not daily basis. People who routinely complain about not having enough time to exercise; or to cook healthy meals; or to play golf; or to read more books; or to visit their elderly parents and other relatives? The list goes on and on. Not having enough time to do the things they actually want to do in life. But given the (hypothetical) opportunity to quit their job with a million dollars, they won't do it! Why on earth not?

Is it simply an effect of the Trap? The compulsion to keep chasing more money – more financial success – on the assumption that with more money comes an automatic improvement in every other aspect of life, so best to keep chasing that money. It's all about *more*! Perhaps it is one of the many manifestations of the cognitive bias that Kahneman unpacks, which seem to almost rule our lives. He unpacks the Prospect Theory and the Loss Aversion bias, consequences of which, Kahneman says, include preference for the *status quo*; and weighting losses far more than gains. Put another way, this is the propensity for the human mind to be swayed far more by potential losses than by similar gains. In this case, the "loss" is the salary. The thought of quitting one's job and the inseparable prospect of losing a salary appears, quite strangely, to weigh heavier on the mind than gaining a million dollars from the lottery. But the prospect of keeping your job and your salary, albeit paid in advance to cover the next

15 years and doing no work, eliminates the loss element. And it sits far more easily with us, even without a million dollars from the lottery. Like I demonstrated – each situation leaves you with a million dollars, more or less, and no job to go to tomorrow, yet we look at them very differently.

Could it just be an inherent, but clearly unfounded in this situation, fear of being broke? Or is it that we have been brainwashed by capitalism from generation to generation. To the extent that we carry mindsets deeply ingrained with the idea that working a 9-5 job for 40 years, and climbing as high up the corporate ladder as you can, is the only acceptable way. And after those 40 years, when you eventually reach retirement, then, and only then, do you qualify to start thinking about hobbies and other pastimes. As for dreams, well, those are for children, aren't they? As we grow up, dreams must be outgrown. Come on… there is more to life than a job! And there is nothing honourable or noble about getting up and going to work for someone else every day. If you must do it, do it. But don't fool yourself into thinking you're doing something honourable.

Like I say in *Corporate Culture Demystified*:[30]

> "The main reason, and in some cases the only reason, that employees get up and go to work every day is to make the other facets of their lives – the facets outside the workplace – better. So, when the demands of the job significantly compromise and adversely af-

fect the quality of life outside the job, what is really going on? Where's the sense in it all?"

Think about that!

Maybe it's just laziness. But wait a minute, how could it be lazy to want to carry on working instead of quitting? Wouldn't quitting be the lazy choice? I'm talking about *mental* laziness. Quitting your job, regardless of circumstance, requires thought, consideration and, ultimately, a decision. Thought and consideration that are not easy and have the effect of necessarily moving people out of their mental comfort zone. And then having to make a decision after all that, well, that's simply too much to handle. Getting up, going to work, pushing papers and dealing with your unsavoury boss becomes a routine. Soon enough there's very little to think about. It becomes robotic. To get out of that robotism and routine requires that hard mental work. It requires some self-assessment and introspection; some serious deliberation. And, at the end of it all, some decision making. And all that is simply too much effort for too many people.

What I've come to notice is that people are averse to making decisions in general. The more important the decision, the more likely it is to be avoided. This, I hypothesize, is for two reasons. The first has been mentioned. Decision-making requires some thinking and mental hard work, and many people are, quite simply, too mentally lazy to do it. But even before coming to a definite decision on whether to quit one's job (or any other meaningful life decision), there is another bigger and more terrifying monster already lurking on the path towards a decision. This is the second reason for this aversion to decision making – fear! People are afraid of making a decision because, aside from the mental effort it requires, they know that the decision may end up being the wrong one. On the face of things, this is understandable and natural. But it all takes a ridiculous turn. You see, a wrong decision – or more accurately, a decision which in hindsight turns out not to have been the best available option at the time that the decision was made – comes with adverse consequences that we can probably handle and even correct just fine. So, in many cases, it is not really the consequences that we're afraid of. Well, not really the *direct* consequences. What we appear to fear most is the indirect consequence of being seen by others to have been "wrong". To be judged unfavourably. What if I quit my job to start my own small business, but it doesn't take off? Then I'll become the laughingstock of my ex-boss, my ex-colleagues and the community in general. What will they say about me? It's far easier and far more attractive an option to simply stick with the *status quo*. Because that allows you to make *no* decision. And when you make no decision, you completely eliminate the possibility of making a bad decision. Nobody can then say you did the wrong thing, because you actually did *no* thing. You just let things pass as they normally do, with the *status quo* remaining well preserved. And nobody – neither yourself nor those people whose opinions you fear – have anything tangible to measure against if you choose not to change. The only measuring stick is the *status quo*, which has remained intact and unchanged. The opposite is true when you make a deliberate decision to deviate from the familiar path you're on. When you actively decide to make a change, everyone, including yourself, has that tangible *status quo* against which to measure your new actively decided and deliberately changed set of circumstances. You open yourself up for every Tom, Dick and Harry to slyly sneer with schadenfreude. And, to make the point again, this is what we appear to fear most.

You can't control other people and their small minds. But you can control the way you deal with those small minds, and you can certainly do a lot to guard against small-mindedness in yourself. Which takes us back to chapter 8 – who are you really trying to impress?

Then there is a less obvious, but more important question. The one that we probably ask ourselves silently, and then quickly hit the mental delete button and pretend the question wasn't asked. If I quit my job, how will I fill my day? It might be an appealing thought, filling your days for a few weeks just as you do on holiday.

But when it becomes every day, every week, every month, every year, it is a burdensome question which necessarily leads to follow up questions like "Is there nothing more to me than my job and the salary it generates?" and "Is that all I exist for?" This can make us feel so shallow and meaningless in the grander scheme of life, that the question is best deleted instantly.

This question, and it's almost instantaneous expungement from the mental record, brings us to a problem so many people live with, often unknowingly. The failure, or worse, *refusal* to find their passion and purpose in life, which we look at in more detail in Part V. Whether you've uncovered it or not, everyone has a purpose and, whatever it may be, I assure you it does not entail working 40 or 50 or 60 hours a week for someone else and in the process enduring the energy-sapping, soul-destroying daily stresses and the weekly Glenroe fever that it invariably brings. No matter how high a salary you receive in return! In fact, the higher the salary, the sooner you are financially able to get yourself out of that trap. But people choose not to escape. People choose to put themselves through the continued grind for more money that they don't need.

I am certainly among the lucky ones who have found their purpose – candidly and practically analysing various facets of life; through my books sharing my thoughts, ideas and philosophies; and, hopefully, inspiring a different way of thinking and acting that will lead to a better life and, with a bit of luck, a better world. I still have my day job because I need to. I need to financially support my family, and I need to pay the costs of publishing my books. They don't generate sufficient income on their own, not yet anyway. But with a million dollars, wow! I would quit my job in an instant and do what I love – write and write and write! And it wouldn't matter if my books generated no income for the next 15 years.

Start looking for your passion and your purpose. And start making a more concerted effort to dedicate some of your time to it, whether you have a million dollars or not. Have a dream and chase that dream! There is a particularly hard-hitting and thought-provoking saying I came across:

> "A salary is the drug they give you to make you forget your dreams."

The circumstances I have presented in the form of winning a million dollars, or being offered Options 1 and 2 are hypothetical, of course. But despite their hypothetical nature, they give you a glimpse into the way you really view your life and the world, particularly in a financial sense. Your thoughts and feelings are real, despite the hypothetical nature of the circumstances presented. Your thoughts and feelings tell you who you are and what is important to you. This question – would you quit your job? – also presents a brilliant illustration of the overall theme of Kahneman's book (*Thinking, Fast and Slow*). People go through life for the most part making completely irrational, nonsensical decisions in pretty much every aspect of life. And what we see in particular – or at least I hope we do – is the way we make irrational decisions that are borne of a deeply ingrained, and often mindless obsession with money. An entrenched mental slavery to money. But the worst of it all is that the decisions we make about money, particularly the accumulation of it, come at a cost.

The cost of chasing more money may not be noticeable on the face of things, but it is real!

CHAPTER 14

THE COST OF MONEY

The way our minds have been attuned and conditioned in this capitalist world is to see money as a cost. As *the* cost. The cost we must pay for various things in life, whether they be needs or desires. But what about the cost of that money? What do we have to pay over in exchange for the acquisition of the money which we will then use to satisfy our needs and desires? Many of us, unfortunately, don't give that aspect a thought. We simply don't look at money that way. We don't realise, or even acknowledge in the slightest, that we are actively paying a certain price for every new dollar we receive. Worse, we *refuse* to see it that way. Money has a cost, and you might be surprised at how high it can be. The pursuit of money eats away at your time, your relationships, your health, and your dreams. In short, it costs you your happiness, and you probably don't even realise it!

Every evening before bedtime I give my children milk and a marshmallow, and we watch 10-20 minutes of a movie. Aside from the fact that this is often the best part of my day, I've come to be quite astonished at how these children's movies so often carry profound messages and lessons for adults. One of the movies we recently watched was *Imagine That*. Eddie Murphy plays a big shot stockbroker with a young daughter whose mother has divorced him. At some stage in the movie, the highly irate ex-wife points out that he actually has two jobs – that of a stockbroker, and that of a father, and it's about time he started giving the necessary attention to the latter. It's a message for every working parent out there. And it is most applicable to those who voluntarily put in more hours at the office to earn more money and bigger promotions that they know they don't really need.

TIME

For the average adult, money is earned through formal employment. That's the way the capitalist world works. But let's look at it through a slightly different lens; a lens that is seldom used. The essence of employment entails people trading their time for money. People are essentially *paying* the employer in a currency called time and, in exchange, they are receiving a pre-agreed monthly quantum of this thing called money. Everyone is familiar with the concept of employment, but perhaps not quite this depiction of it. And the reason is simple. It is because time is so seldom seen as something of any meaningful value, let alone the priceless value it should command. I often say that time is the most precious, yet most undervalued commodity we all have.

You see, unlike money, time is a resource that can never be recovered or replaced. When you give away an hour of your time, it is gone forever. And we only have 24 hours a day. 24 hours that must be used wisely and allocated fairly to the different shades of our lives, each outlined by the various relationships we have – children, spouse, parents, and the oft forgotten relationship we have – or *should* have – with ourselves. The more time you spend trying to acquire more money, the less time you have available for all the important aspects of your life. Like I said, it's like accounting. When one facet of your life is credited with an extra hour, there is another facet that suffers the consequence and must be debited with that hour. Time, to repeat, is a great equaliser, because unlike the relative value of a dollar to a millionaire v Average Joe, an hour is always an hour. You can't get more of them, no matter who you are.

Yet we just don't seem to realise this. We routinely trade, no, we routinely *pay* more and more of our time in exchange for money. Worse, the amount of money we receive in the form of a salary often stays the same while we pay over more and more of our time by working extra hours, taking work home and all the usual formal employment "norms". Every employee, at some point, works extra hours outside their contractual obligation without receiving a dollar more than their contractual salary. Okay, let's call it an advance purchase if you like. Pay more time today, and at the end of the year I might get that promotion and the higher salary that comes with it. So far it sounds quite logical. But guess what any promotion comes with? Higher responsibility, higher stress levels and, almost invariably, an *even higher* number of hours. Yet a promotion is universally viewed as a major positive with little consideration for the added price you pay for it.

RELATIONSHIPS

Let's dig deeper. As we hand over more and more of our time, assumingly in the quest to get a promotion and the higher salary that comes with it, we're leaving ourselves with less hours to spare for other things outside this act of earning more money. We all realise this on some level but we tell ourselves, or rather convince ourselves, that the additional money (and, of course, the things it will be able to buy) will outweigh the reduced hours we have available outside our employment requirements. But it's not just reduced time that we're dealing with. It is *reduced time available for important relationships*. We internally rationalise. We convince ourselves that there is an end game. That we will, soon enough, reach this destination called "enough money", at which point we can take a step back, breathe, and fully enjoy all the fruits of our labour. Kahneman has already given us the Magic Number that objectively constitutes "enough", but the reality is that "enough" seldom, if ever, really exists in the human mind. If it did, there would be no such thing as a billionaire. We always want more because money, and the status and power it brings, is a drug. The more we have the more we want. And we rationalise further.

I came across the most profound social media post from a Catholic priest in Zimbabwe whom I have known since childhood, Father Isaac. As he unpacks a Biblical parable, he explains that more money gives us more options. This, of course, is an objective truth we cannot get away from. He believes that we – human beings – like having more options which translate to more power, and places us in a position akin to that of God. But Father Isaac goes on to explain that we – human beings – were not created to possess such power and possibilities *alone*. No, on the contrary, we were created for each other. For relationship and community. Money takes us in the opposite direction. It takes us towards greater independence and less interdependence. It allows us to do as we please, with little or no recourse to the help or even opinion of others. If you think about it, this really sums up so much of what is wrong with the world!

Here's the most profound part: Money and human relationships are inversely proportional to one another.

> "The more money I have, the less need there is for human relationships; while the less

> money I have, the more trust and investment I have in human relationships."

This may suggest that more money automatically equals less trust and investment in human relationships. That is, of course, not the case. And I would go as far as saying that was never the intended message behind Father Isaac's post. Rather, the point is to demonstrate what money *can* do and at what cost it *can* come. The further point is to arm readers with this knowledge in the hope that they consciously avoid this particular danger that lurks ahead.

Moving away from theological explanations to something more secular, Warren Buffet seems to say something very similar. And the fact that it is coming from one of the wealthiest people in the world serves to confirm that money does not and does not have to automatically equal less trust and less investment in human relations. In a presentation he gave at the University of Georgia[31], Buffet is said to have summed up the measure of success, particularly as you near the end of your life, as "the number of people you want to have love you, (who) actually do love you."

Buffet went on to elaborate, "I know people who have a lot of money, and they get testimonial dinners and they get hospital wings named after them. But the truth is that nobody in the world loves them. If you get to my age and nobody thinks well of you, I don't care how big your bank account is, your life is a disaster. The problem with love is that it's not for sale. The only way to get love is to be lovable. It's very irritating if you have a lot of money. You'd like to think you could write a check: I'll buy a million dollars' worth of love. But it doesn't work that way. The more you give love away, the more you get."

This reminds me of Malcolm Gladwell's *Roseto Mystery*.[32] Roseto is a town in Pennsylvania, populated entirely by generational immigrants from a small town in Italy by the same name. As Gladwell's account goes, a doctor called Stewart Wolf stumbled upon this community and the fact that nobody there died of heart disease. He ran tests over a period of years. He and his team looked at every possible factor to establish the reason behind this community having a death rate three times lower than the rest of the United States. It was not their diet. They didn't have any particularly healthy diet. It was not their exercise. They did none. It was not their genetics. There were relatives of these people, from the same genetic line who had since moved to other parts of the United States. It was not the geographical location – the people in the two closest towns, one less than a mile away and the other less than six miles away, were different. So, what was it? It was the community. To say it was their way of life wouldn't really answer any questions. It was their *social* way of life. Their relationships with each other!

After five or ten years of financial success (at the expense of the important relationships in our life) we tell ourselves that we're now so good at doing what we do, it would make no sense at all to stop. And as we now know, when you don't give a relationship sufficient time it will weaken, break and eventually die. And when that happens, all the money in the world will not resuscitate it. All that is left is regret.

YOUR DREAMS

There is a dreamer in everyone! Of this I am certain. The unfortunate reality of life is that, far too often, the size of the dreamer within us decreases as we age. Every child has a big dreamer within them, regardless of what the dream itself may be. Up to a certain age, nothing is impossible! As we get older, however, life and societal norms and conditioning kick in and begin to suffocate that dreamer more and more. We finish school, maybe go to university, and ultimately land up in a job of some sort. Ideally a "good job". After all, that's what every parent wants for their child, right? Maybe we climb the corporate ladder. Because, again, that's just what people do! More pertinently, that's what *successful* people do. There is also the not so small consideration that our parents, after having put us through primary, secondary and tertiary schooling have met our every need through all those years, and are simply not prepared, or even equipped, to continue supporting us while we chase our dream as twenty somethings. As far as they and our global capitalist society are concerned, dreaming is for children. For adults, it's all about real life. And real-life entails getting a job. And then we ourselves become parents, and that parent in us immediately gets in on the dream-suffocating act. After all, our dreams will not provide for our family's immediate needs. The dreams we once had as children, and the dreamers within us, slowly but surely fade away into the distance, leaving only a trail of *what ifs* and regrets.

As the saying goes: "Either you're working on your own dreams, or you're working on someone else's." The latter is exactly what any formal job is. You get up and go to work every day, dedicating a third of your life (probably more) to that job, and for what? To get a salary that is probably not commensurate with everything you put in and put up with but, more importantly, to bring your employer's dreams to fruition. What about *your own dreams?* Do they not mean anything in *your own life?* If you hadn't noticed, this is yet another manifestation of the Trap! It is perhaps worth repeating the saying that was shared in the previous chapter:

> "A salary is the drug they give you to make you forget your dreams".

HEALTH

It's worth repeating that time is life's great equaliser. No matter who you are and what you do, you will only ever have 24 hours each day. And you are human, so no matter how much money you have, and how much *more* money you are about to make, your human body has physiological needs – mental and physical – that cannot be abandoned. Let's start with sleep. "Burning the midnight oil" is a common phenomenon, worsened by this technological age we live in where employees are expected to be reachable at all hours. Literally. In one of my previous jobs the CEO went as far as spelling it out in a management meeting, that everyone had been given a company cell phone and was expected to be reachable at all times. The looks around the table were priceless, but nobody said a word, which was testament to the toxic culture. I was, thankfully, about to leave that job otherwise I may well have said more than I should have.

What about seven to eight hours' sleep? What about exercise? We know that we need these things, but we rationalise the fact that we are not getting enough of either. We tell ourselves that we don't *really* need to have that much sleep. That we'll be okay without exercising every day. After all, half the office is in far worse shape than I am anyway. I'm actually in decent shape for my age. And so, willingly, we pay over our health in exchange for more money.

Let's go back to the Gallup survey and its overarching finding that 85% of the estimated one billion full time employees globally "hate their job and especially their boss". What this means is that something in the region of 850 million people get up every day and put themselves through eight to ten hours of misery, all in the name of money. What must this do to a person's frame of mind, not only during those long, unpleasant hours at work, but also when they get home after eight to ten hours of misery? When they are supposed to be spending quality, happy time with their families? Is that even possible in that state of mind? They can't be mentally at ease because their mind is indefinitely compromised. They cannot fully let go of all the crap that has happened during the working day, and all that will follow tomorrow. How must this affect a person's mental health?

Years down the line, money will buy you the best medical treatment available. But it won't buy you your health back. There is a difference. Ask yourself who is better off, who is more successful, and who is happier – the person who can afford to, and does, receive the best medical treatment; or the person who doesn't need any medical treatment? Here's a profound, hard-hitting quote I came across.

> "If you don't make time for your health, you will be forced to make time for your illness."

But let's face it, many people have little choice. Everyone needs money to meet the needs of themselves and their families, which is the foundation for happiness. I cannot overstate that. For many, doing the job they do is a matter of necessity. The message is for those who have options. Whether it is the option to go into early semi-retirement on the foundation of "enough" of a financial platform, or to take a lower-paying and, consequently, lower-stress job that can still meet your needs fairly comfortably. As we know, the more stress one has, the lower their Happiness Score will be. When you go to a job that you hate every day, purely for the purpose of earning money, the cost of that money is your happiness! You have to keep performing a self-check. You have to keep asking yourself whether the stress of your job is worth it. Or whether you'd be happier in a lower-paying and lower-stress job.

All of these facets of life – relationships, health, regret – directly impact the state of our lives and, in short, our happiness. Which brings us to one of life's great paradoxes. While we go out chasing more money on the blind and foolish assumption that it will bring with it more happiness, that very act – the act of chasing money – is slowly but surely costing us our happiness.

There is a well-known axiom about selling one's soul to the devil. And in writing this chapter I have come to realise its real-life meaning, and I believe we all go through life doing it on various levels. Your soul comprises your dreams, your purpose and your over-all happiness. The devil, on the other hand, is represented by money. We all sell our souls to the devil on some level, albeit unconsciously for the most part. It's time to become consciously aware of what we're doing. Every time we push aside the thought of pursuing our dreams and our purpose in the name of earning more money, we're selling off a small part of our soul.

There are questions that need to be answered, and you're the only person that can fully answer them. But in order come up with any answers, you first have to ask yourself the questions!

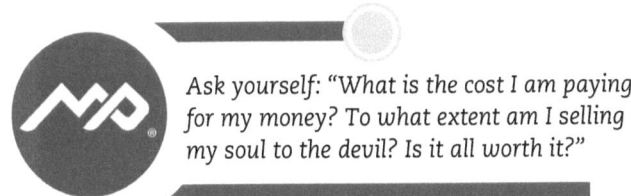

Ask yourself: "What is the cost I am paying for my money? To what extent am I selling my soul to the devil? Is it all worth it?"

CHAPTER 15

PEACE OF MIND

We've reached the final chapter of this part of the book – Money – which I have found so utterly fascinating as I wrote it. This thing called money; all it stands for; all it is (and isn't); and all it does (and doesn't do). Negativity has taken much of the limelight in the preceding chapters, and I now find myself compelled to conclude this part of the book on a positive note. Failure to off-set all the negatives, at least partially, with something of substantial positivity would render me an idealist and a Utopian romantic. It would render the messages within this book merely theoretical. I am not those things, and the messages and ideas in this book are intended for practical application in day-to-day life and the very real pursuit of happiness.

This may be the most opportune moment to point out that while some of the themes of this part of the book are, admittedly, theoretical on the face of things – "What would you do if you won the lottery?" and "Would you quit your job?" – they have a much bigger and more practical role. The thoughts that these theoretical questions illicit are real thoughts that betray the real way our respective minds work. They tell us a lot about who we are; the ideals we have; the value we think money carries; and the meaning it has in our lives. Our *real* lives. And the way we think about money certainly does guide many of the choices we *actually* make in life.

We're not fools. We know things which we don't know that we know, but we know them anyway. We don't realise it, but we know on some level that there is a distinction between pleasure and happiness; that happiness is really the goal, and not pleasure. This is why we default to "I will invest" when posed with the prospect of winning a million dollars because the alternative – which is to go and spend it on the most wonderful of pleasures – does not get us any closer to the goal of happiness. It should, perhaps be re-stated – I think we know this without realising that we know it.

Let's get back to what I see as the single most valuable role money plays in life. Consider this thing called *peace of mind*. It's a two-part term, made up of *peace* and *the mind*. It's more about the latter than it is about former. Peace is a broad concept, and physical peace is what most readily comes to mind in the form of absence of war and physical violence or threat of violence. But the human mind is a complex thing, and an even more complex and weird *place* where thoughts and ideas reside, grow and often run riot. A place that can quickly become far removed from the realms of reality. Anything, literally anything, can exist there. And amongst that *anything*, there are demons and monsters that must be tamed before they run amok and create wars of their own that will be fought daily in the mind. Wars that will inevitably spill over from the realms of the mind into reality at any given moment in the form of our mood, our demeanour and our general attitude towards people, situations and life in general.

There are people who value power and status more than peace of mind. There are people who value another billion dollars more than peace of mind. And that is part of the cost they pay for their money because, as we know, there is always a cost. But you and I, who go about life merely trying to earn a decent, comfortable living for ourselves and our families, we want peace. We want physical peace, which is obvious. But we also want mental peace. We want an existence that is not characterised by mental stress, anxiety and worry, regardless of how realistic or unrealistic the things causing that mental stress are. This is peace of mind.

WHAT IF?

These demons and monsters that lurk in the mind often take the form of *what ifs*. Many of them are highly unlikely to become reality, yet still they lurk. And they grow over time.

Let's go back to The Million Dollar question and, in particular, the first ten days during which pretty much everyone was happy to park their winnings in the bank until they came up with a concrete investment plan. This demonstrates that the immediate value of a one-million-dollar windfall, (or any amount of money that substantially exceeds the financial cost of our short-term needs) to pretty much everyone, lies not in the ability to *immediately* withdraw or utilise it in any way.

Knowing what the immediate value of a large sum of money is *not*, doesn't really help us as much as knowing what the immediate value *is*. And there must, surely, be *some* immediate value or benefit that a substantial amount of money would bring, even if it is merely parked in an investment and remains untouched. We cannot realistically say that suddenly having an extra million dollars will not have any instantly positive effect at all. Impossible! And it is this unseen and unspoken effect that represents the biggest value of money – peace of mind. *Immediate* peace of mind!

It is most fitting that money, in all its illusory glory and attraction, represents the antidote to the almost equally illusory *what ifs* that occupy and burden the adult mind far more than they should. The greatest value that money brings (beyond meeting our needs) is its ability to extinguish other illusions – illusions of things that *might* happen, which, in turn, cause untold anxiety and stress. Money provides a comforting answer to those *what if's* that we go through adult life continually asking ourselves, and continually stressing about when we don't have a satisfactory answer readily at hand. What if I lose my job and I can't support my family? What if I, or a family member, needs major surgery that our medical plan does not cover? You see, these things may happen, but it is probably more likely that they will not happen. And deep down, we know that. But reality takes a backseat, as it often does in so many facets of life, and we allow *what ifs* that may never come to pass to negatively impact our state of mind in the here and now. Money sitting in the bank, in its highly illusory form, serves to counteract the negative impact of those what ifs. It gives us a greater ability to cast them aside, and with them the associated fear, anxiety and other negative emotions. This means, quite simply, a higher Happiness Score!

It doesn't end there. Money can also be *actively* used to eliminate some of those *what ifs*. Prevention is better than cure, wisdom tells us. I had a recent experience which perfectly demonstrates this principle in a manner anyone can identify with. It was about six months ago, and I was on a business trip from Bahrain to Harare. Covid-related travel restrictions had begun to ease, and it was the first opportunity I had in over two years to visit my brother and his family in Johannesburg. His family included a beautiful baby girl who was already 18 months old, and whom I had never met. So I booked a whistlestop weekend trip from Saturday morning to Monday afternoon. This would allow me the full weekend with the family, and Monday morning to spend on my own, having breakfast and writing for a few hours at my favourite spot for that in South Africa – Mugg and Bean.

Sunday was soon upon us, and after the morning church service I went straight to get a PCR test done for my flight the following day. I had been told by my brother that the place down the road does tests in a matter of hours. When I got there, not only was I told that I would *not* get the result that day, but I was told that they could not even guarantee a result before lunchtime the following day. This was because it was a Sunday and test samples would not be sent to the laboratory until mid-morning the following day, Monday. This would have been cutting things really fine with my flight at 4pm.

I decided to look into other options, and eventually learned of a mobile testing van at the airport that guaranteed test results in an hour. The catch? Aside from the comparatively much longer drive, it was double the price. But I paid it. I *happily* paid it. Of course my brother and several other people were horrified – "How could you pay an extra ZAR750?" I was asked several times over. My answer was simple – My peace of mind is worth far, far more than ZAR750 (about US$50). What that extra ZAR750 did was allow me to completely enjoy that Sunday afternoon with my brother and his family; and my Monday morning writing session at Mugg and Bean without this PCR issue hanging over my head. I felt completely comfortable and at ease in the knowledge that I would board my flight without any complications and late surprises. And the cost of that comfort – that peace of mind – was a mere fifty dollars. In the grander scheme of things, that is a bargain!

Money can actively buy you peace of mind in various forms and at various costs. You can engage a security company to patrol your yard at night so you can sleep more easily. You can move to a new, safer neighbourhood where the rent is double what you were paying. But your peace of mind is more than twice as valuable. Or you can buy a new car because you're so tired of stressing about an inevitable breakdown every time you get into your old jalopy to go anywhere.

Money can buy peace of mind, which increases the Happiness Score. If it is used wisely!

WHAT'S REALLY IMPORTANT TO YOU?

While money allows us to cast aside many *what ifs*, we shouldn't discard them completely. They contain nuggets of wisdom we can use. You see, camouflaged within those frightening *what ifs* that keep us up at night, are the things that are important to us in reality. In the here and now. They are the things that prompt us to ask these *what ifs* in the first place. You see, when you ask, "what if I can no longer support my family?" it is clear that your family and their wellbeing is of paramount importance in your life. Likewise, you reveal the importance of your health when you ask, "What if I need surgery?" It is in this sense that those *what if*'s must be taken notice of. They should be seen as pointers to the things that we value most in life. And when we become consciously aware of the things we value most in life, a couple of things should happen:

- We should develop a greater and more deliberate sense of gratitude for those things, which feeds into the gratitude list from chapter 2; and
- We should make a bigger effort to dedicate more time to those things. Using the examples above, this would simply mean spending more time with your family; and on activities that benefit your health.

We looked at the essence and value of time, so I won't go into it again in much detail. Suffice to say that it represents the second big value of money. Quite simply, it allows you to use your time better. It allows you to use your time more freely. It allows you to do the things you *choose* to do with your time rather than giving countless extra, unrewarded and most importantly unnecessary hours to your employer because you are so wholly financially dependent on your job, that you have no choice.

To wrap up this chapter and this part of the book, I leave you with a thought I'd like you to seriously reflect on:

Money is not a goal in itself. The accumulation of money for the sake of accumulating money – aside from costing you your time, relationships, health, dreams and overall happiness – is just silly. Money is a tool, and just like any other tool – from a hammer to a power drill – money can work wonders if used properly. But it can also cause untold pain and injury if used improperly.

Money is the tool that can help you achieve peace of mind; and can give you the freedom to concentrate more of your time on the things that mean the most to you in life. Use it wisely.

PART V
SUCCESS

CHAPTER 16
WILL THE REAL SUCCESS PLEASE STAND UP

Let me begin by repeating the first few paragraphs of a chapter entitled "What is success?" from my first book, Life Demystified:[33]

> "A question that has puzzled and bedevilled humankind throughout the ages and will undoubtedly continue to do so – as the concept is so elusive and so subjective – is: What is success?
>
> I have trawled through countless articles on the topic and considered a plethora of definitions. These range from the somewhat simplistic, such as Richard Branson's quip that 'Success is measured by how happy you are'; to the highly cryptic: 'Success is understanding that you cannot keep what you don't give away' (of unknown provenance); to the flippant and forgettable: 'Success is remembering to balance work with passion' (author also unknown).
>
> The highly subjective nature of 'success' and the efforts already mounted by thousands of people to define it does not absolve me of what I see as my duty, by virtue of writing this

book, at least to attempt to give it a meaning or definition that can be widely accepted. After all, revealing the secret to success becomes a pointless exercise if there is no generally accepted definition of the concept of success.

So, after laboriously scouring the internet and pondering the various definitions, I eventually concluded that the very first definition that came up in a Google search was not only the simplest, but also the most accurate:

"The accomplishment of an aim or purpose."

I liked the two-pronged definition incorporating an aim or a purpose at the time I first encountered it and now, some four years later, though my views on the concept of success have become somewhat more refined, I still find this definition highly applicable. That notwithstanding, I have grown to find immense appreciation for Richard Branson's aforementioned definition, which I had previously labelled simplistic, and which will be revisited as the chapter progresses.

"Success is measured by how happy you are."

"The accomplishment of an aim or purpose" reconciles perfectly with my view that there are two separate and distinct forms of success that we can experience. The first entails finding and living your purpose, which is what I call ultimate success. There can be no more fulfilling and content existence than that. But to get there almost invariably means taking the more difficult path at first. The path that is more difficult, not forever, but *at first!* This is consistent with a well-established and accepted principle of life in general – nothing worth having comes easily. The unfortunate reality, however, is that many people never find or live out their purpose, whether by choice or otherwise. I go into great detail on the concept of *purpose* in the chapters that follow.

Not everyone finds their purpose. Not everyone *wants* to find their purpose. Of those who do find it, not everyone chooses to make it their life, and that's all okay. My intention is neither to force people to find their purpose, nor to castigate them when they can't or won't. My intention, rather, is to share my views in the hope of provoking thought (at worst) and providing inspiration (at best). Ultimately, whatever I share must be considered and applied (or not applied) in the context of each person's individual circumstances and preferences. Noam Chomsky put it perfectly:

> "Reading a book does not mean just turning pages. It means thinking about it, identifying parts that you want to go back to, asking how to place it in a broader context, pursuing the ideas. Reading a book is an intellectual exercise which

> stimulates thought, questions, imagination."*

Does this mean that anyone who hasn't found and isn't living their purpose cannot be considered successful? And, perhaps more importantly, cannot be happy? Absolutely not! Millions of people live happy and fulfilling lives without having found their purpose. Many have managed to find their purpose, or have inadvertently stumbled upon it, yet they choose *not* to pursue it, opting instead to remain in the comfort zone. Like I said, that's perfectly ok. Whether you have found your purpose or not; and if you have, whether you've chosen to pursue it or not, there is still the second form of success. It comes through the achievement of the goals that we set for ourselves. This is the "aim" part of the two-pronged definition we looked at. The key is to set goals that, when achieved, make our lives better in one way or another. Goals that have the effect of reducing the stress in our lives and, consequently, increasing our Happiness Score.

To go back to an example from the previous chapter – a goal should not be to have X amount of money. Think ahead. Think seriously about what you would like to do with that money if and when you have managed to accumulate it. Perhaps you've longed to move to a safer neighbourhood.

---

* Scrolling through my social media, I came across a photograph of a page from a book, capturing this quote. I have been unable to establish the name of the book itself.

To reiterate, then, the goal is *not* to have X amount of money but, rather, it is to move to a safer neighbourhood. The additional money is what you require to meet the mortgage deposit or the higher rental. Money, then, becomes a critical success factor in the achievement of the goal, rather than the goal itself. This is an important distinction.

A goal should also be something that increases your Happiness Score. At the time of setting your goal ask yourself if it is, in fact, something that will increase your Happiness Score. And that means over a sustained period as opposed to a sudden, once off, rush of dopamine. Because that, as we know, is pleasure, not happiness. Let's stick with the goal of moving to a safer neighbourhood. Will it increase my happiness score? It would appear quite obvious that moving from an unsafe neighbourhood to a safe one will undoubtedly remove, or at least significantly reduce, the inescapable stress occasioned by living in daily fear for the safety of yourself and your family. That increases your Happiness Score, and it does so over a sustained period.

Some goals, like saving up for a move to a safe neighbourhood, take a long time to accomplish. But there are other goals – short terms goals that still positively impact our Happiness Score – that represent low hanging fruits in the quest for success and happiness. The quick wins if you like (and we all do like the odd quick win). Look for them and grab them! Many of these come in the form of habits, although habits, of course, must first be developed. As we unpacked in chapter 4, you really can make yourself happier by deciding to do exactly that. By deciding to change your habits in such a way as to reduce the stress that you visit upon yourself. At first reading it seems obvious, but upon further reflection, the words of Duhigg become more and more profound: "To modify a habit, you must *decide* to change it."[34] We should probably take this a step backwards for completeness. In order to make the decision to change a habit, you must first identify and acknowledge the existence, nature and extent of the habit that must be changed.

Set goals to develop better habits that in turn will improve your state of mind. We looked at some of them in previous chapters. Why wouldn't you make a concerted effort to leave home 10 minutes earlier each morning? It would undoubtedly reduce your stress in traffic and improve your mood for the day. Or make a habit of leaving your car key in one specific place, so that when you're ready to walk out the door each morning, you do so in a state of calm as opposed to a state of stress because you've had to go back and spend three or four minutes hunting for that key. Three or four all-important minutes that have not been budgeted for in your morning routine, and which represent the difference between beating the traffic jam and getting caught in it.

That misplaced car key, and those few minutes it takes to find it, can significantly impact your stress levels and your mood for the next three or four hours! And, of course, your Happiness Score. Developing such simple habits represent quick and immediate wins in the quest to simply be happier. Every single day!

The reality, if we care to face it, is that we are all very aware of most of our bad habits. We are equally aware of the way those bad habits negatively impact us (and others). But we cast all that aside, to the deepest darkest corner of our minds where it can cause the least interference. And we "happily" carry on as we were. This backdrop gives Duhigg's assertion the significance and importance it deserves. It demonstrates that what appears obvious and perhaps easy, is quite the opposite. Recognising and acknowledging (to ourselves at least) our bad habits is something we all do. But taking that recognition and acknowledgement and turning it into a decision to change is something very different.

I retain the view that your purpose is your ultimate success. And it is my hope that the following two chapters will help people to find and live theirs. At the very least, I hope to provide food for serious thought, and perhaps plant a seed. But the majority of the global population doesn't live a purpose-driven life. To pretend otherwise is just silly. The *real* success (as opposed to *ultimate* success), cannot be something that applies to the minority. To understand *real* success, we must go back to Richard Branson's definition:

Success is measured by your happiness!

I have revisited this definition, and in particular my reasons for labelling it, quite unfairly and erroneously in hindsight, simplistic. I can only think it was because it leaves two fundamental questions unanswered. What is the measure of happiness? And how is it calculated? I believe I have since found the answers to these questions and, in so doing, have been able to see the value of the definition. The measure and calculation of the concept called *happiness* is, of course, the Happiness Score!

Those previously unanswered questions, in a way, provide the foundation to debunk the myth that has been perpetuated from generation to generation. The myth that money is the measure – the *only* measure – of success. The myth that more money equals greater success, regardless of what you are doing in life; whether or not you get any real satisfaction from it; and, of course, the cost you are paying for that money. This, as we should well recognise by now, is the Trap! While this mindset is as unfortunate as it is erroneous, it somewhat makes sense when you consider that money provides the easiest, most consistent and most globally acceptable unit of measure in life. That mindset, and the easy measurability of money, is so deeply ingrained in us to the extent that even such influential people as Robin Sharma can come to the conclusion that he, himself, was "successful but miserable".

Money, indeed, is a consistent and objective unit of measure. There can be no argument, misunderstanding or doubt about that. *What* it actually measures is where a fundamental misunderstanding lies and where valid arguments not only exist and can be made, but *must* be raised. Money measures one's financial standing, commonly known these days as net worth. Nothing more, nothing less. It measures neither success, nor happiness. So many of us dedicate enormous amounts of time, energy and focus on our careers. Getting the next professional certification, the next promotion, and of course, the next pay rise. We routinely set these goals, but for what, really? To get an ego boost from a more elaborate and important-sounding job title, and to smile about a bigger salary and a bigger bank balance that we don't really know what to do with? Does any of this make us happier on a day-to-day basis?

The real success – the day-to-day success – that routinely impacts our lives is not measured in money. It is measured in happiness!

CHAPTER 17

PATH AND PURPOSE

What is purpose, or life-purpose? Does the concept exist at all? And if it exists, does it have practical application in real life or is it merely an abstract idea pushed by utopians?

Like I said in the previous chapter, these are questions I cannot answer for you. Nobody can, except yourself. What I can do – which this chapter *will* do – is share my thoughts and ideas and put forward my own answers to the questions posed. But it is *my* way of thinking. They are *my* answers which have been shaped by *my* life experiences thus far; *my* life circumstances at present (which, indeed, are subject to change at any given moment); *my* values and *my* ideals. They will certainly not be shared by all and sundry, nor should they be. What they should do is plant a seed. And that seed should grow into a serious and deliberate thought process about this thing called *purpose*. A thought process that many have never consciously undertaken. Whatever conclusion you then arrive at is not as important as the fact that you have arrived there through clear and informed thinking. And, with a bit of luck, thinking that is slightly different from what is often the mindless norm. Until I set about writing my first book some four to five years ago, I was one of those people who refused to think any differently from what I thought I knew and, more particularly, what I thought I knew was important. I was one of those people who had never given a conscious thought to this concept of life-purpose. It was unimportant, if it existed at all.

    I came out of law school and, in line with what I thought I knew, the obvious and inescapable next step was – and had to be – straight into legal practice. I got a job with one of the leading law firms in Harare, where I would stay for the next four years. At no point – neither before nor during law school; and at no stage during my four-year stint in private practice – did I ever think to myself "Ah, this is my purpose in life." Other thoughts did cross my mind, though. Purpose or no purpose, I *did* think that this was the *path* I was supposed to be on. To put things into perspective, and to demonstrate the (low) calibre of my thinking, let's bear in mind I didn't know any other path. I was essentially comparing my present path to nothing. There could only be one winner. In my second year with the firm, there was a farewell party for the senior partner, who had been with the firm for 50 years. It's now 18 years ago, but I vividly remember the day, and what was at the time a priceless photo I had taken with this supremely respected and experienced man, the now late William Turpin (affectionately known to all as Dick Turpin). Suddenly, this was not only the path I was supposed to be on. It was the path that I *would*, again, almost inescapably, be on until retirement. I told myself, with an air of resolve and certainty, that this would be me in another 50 years' time.

There I was, envisioning myself at that firm 50 years into the future, yet there were aspects of being an attorney that I didn't like. No, there were aspects of being an attorney that I absolutely loathed. And I was well aware of that on a conscious level. With the benefit of hindsight, however, I now realise that I had subconsciously conditioned my mind and structured my thinking in such a way that it assigned greater weighting to the aspects that I liked, compared to those that I did not. I told myself that I was on this path, and it was the path upon which I would continue for the next 50 years, because that's just the way it goes. And, of course, because I didn't know anything else. A brilliant illustration of the profound saying "you don't know what you don't know". In my mind and in my own little bubble of reality, that was my path – my only path. And that is the key word – *path*.

At any given point in time, every person is on a path of some sort, whether a good path or not, whether by choice or by force of circumstance. What seems to skip our minds, particularly with regard to career paths, is that the path you are on at any given time is not a life sentence. There are other possible paths. You can change your career if you want to. You can make a decision to step off your current path onto a new one. A new path that leads to a new, more desirable, more purpose-orientated destination. It may not be easy, but the point is that you can do it, and whether or not you do is your choice.

In many cases you will face resistance, not only from yourself and the part of you that is content in the comfort zone, but from your family. When I left private practice (yes, the 50-year path which I thought was engraved in my destiny didn't quite materialise), certain family members were not only disappointed, but openly disapproving. They were very firmly of the view that I had gone to law school and become an attorney, and that that was what I had signed up for. For life! To step off that path was taboo. It was something to be frowned upon. And it *was*, indeed, frowned upon by some. I couldn't really begrudge them because those sentiments mirrored my own from not long before. Despite these disapproving comments and even lectures, I did what I had to do. And that was ultimately the determining factor – I *had to* do it. Necessity prevailed, as it always does and always will. Under different circumstances, I probably wouldn't have considered moving off that path, and if I had considered it, I might well have buckled under the pressure of those disapproving family members.

Fast forward six years and I was working

for one of the biggest companies in the country, heading its Legal Department. Very quickly, just as I had done at Dick Turpin's farewell, I envisioned myself retiring at this company. Those visions soon became more elaborate as the scope of my work expanded from the purely legal realm into one that necessitated a certain level of business acumen. I would retire at that company, I told myself, but as its CEO! This is another very clear illustration of the propensity we have to confine our aspirations to what lies along the path we're already travelling. As I look back, it is with an element of embarrassment at how fickle I was. How I was so easily swayed to re-formulate career and life goals based purely on the path I found myself on at a given moment. It was during my stint with this company that I had my epiphany and found my purpose. I've been a completely different person ever since.

When I left private practice it was solely because of the complete economic meltdown in Zimbabwe in 2007 and 2008. The unreal inflation rates, which saw prices of goods doubling in the space of a day, rendered my Zimbabwe Dollar salary practically worthless. My last pay cheque in that job was equivalent to less than US$40. I left out of sheer financial necessity rather than any sudden desire for change. That economic meltdown was one of what I call life's nudges. You see, if left to our own devices, the default setting is to go with the easiest option. And in most cases, the easiest option is to simply do nothing, as we touched on in chapter 13. That means coasting along on the same old path you're on, which is most probably situated in what has become your comfort zone. Life, the universe and God are only too well aware of this default setting. And so these nudges that life throws up from time to time, which almost invariably take the form of obstacles and difficulties in the short term, are necessary to get us off our current path and onto a better one. Whether we budge or not, these nudges will keep coming! In the words of Orison Swett Marden, and later recounted to us by Tom Butler-Bowdon:[35]

> "Nature will chip and pound us
> remorselessly to bring out our possibilities."

In *Life Demystified*, I go into a lot more detail on life's nudges that have come my way. From my expulsion from school at age 14; to the economic meltdown in Zimbabwe that knocked me off the path to becoming the next Dick Turpin; and several other nudges that represent watershed moments in my life. These nudges that I experienced had the effect of forcing me off a particular path that I was on at the time, and onto a new one. A new path that didn't appear to be a better one at the time but was a necessary one. It is only with the benefit of hindsight, that I can see that the new paths onto which I was nudged have, indeed, been better ones. Without the element of necessity that laced those nudges that life threw at me, I may well have missed out on several new, exciting and life-changing paths. Each one of these nudges represented a small step towards ultimately uncovering my purpose: to capture my thoughts, ideas and analyses of life in the books I write, and to share them with the world in the hope that they will inspire a different way of thinking and acting that will, in turn, lead to a better life and a better world.

    A path is different to a purpose. A purpose is something powerful. Something compelling. It is a journey – a fantastic, enjoyable, fulfilling, rewarding, gratifying journey! Importantly, it may well be (and often is) something completely different to the path you find yourself on. But we don't see it. We don't even look for it. To repeat the words I say to my children almost daily, you're not going to see something if you're not looking for it. Perhaps we don't want to look for it because we fear we might actually find it, and then what? That prospect can be far too scary. It might mean that we actually need to consider getting off the current path. And we might like the current path a little too much to want to get off it. The current path might well represent our comfort zone, while the path leading to your purpose may appear to be the more difficult option. This is an opportune moment to share Farrah Gray's now-famous observation which, as I reflect on my own life choices, rings so very true for me:

"Comfort is the enemy of achievement."

To search for, to find, and to live out your purpose is undoubtedly the more difficult path in life. At first anyway. But it is also the more fulfilling path. The *completely* fulfilling path I might say.

Human beings can be strange creatures. In so many instances we know very well what we would like to have; why we would like to have it (which includes both superficial and meaningful reasons); and what we need to do to get it. Perhaps the most common and easily identifiable example for the vast majority of the global population, is to want a better physique. A six-pack to flaunt on social media (because that's a priority in this in this age we live in). We want it, and we know perfectly well how to get it. Aside from the obvious narcissistic motivation, we also know very well – whether consciously or subconsciously – that a better physique will necessarily bring with it all sorts of other objectively meaningful and positive effects, most notably better physical health and better mental health through improved self-esteem and the hormones that physical exercise release. But we settle for something less. We reconcile ourselves to a flabby stomach because it is simply too hard to put in the necessary exercise and make the necessary dietary changes. We rationalise. We make excuses for ourselves. We downright lie to ourselves so that we can choose the easier path.

The same principle applies to life purpose. Whilst not as patently obvious as the benefits of weight loss, we would (theoretically) like to find and live out our life purpose. But the requisite inputs and sacrifices are, quite simply, off-putting. And so, we settle. We reconcile ourselves to a non-purpose driven life with the consolation that, in the grander scheme of things, life is still good. Perhaps even better in the sense that life is there to be enjoyed rather than spent working so hard to find this thing called purpose, if it even exists at all. Again, we rationalise. We make excuses. We lie to ourselves! And then we regret it when it's too late.

Digressing slightly, but it must be said, I find it both interesting and flabbergasting the way we routinely assess the cost of self-improvement – in its numerous forms – to be too high, but never give a thought to the cost of the money that we mindlessly chase. We instinctively tell ourselves things like "I can't cut out an hour of TV and do some exercise because my work days are so taxing that I deserve some down time" or "I can't curb my drinking habits because then I'll probably have to stop meeting up with my friends and it's important to meet up with friends." Yet somehow we *don't* think "I can't keep putting in these extra hours at the office because it will be detrimental to my relationships with my spouse and children." Crazy, right? It's like we don't care about ourselves and what's really good for us.

One fairly common rationalisation that I've heard is "It's my life purpose to be the best parent to my child(ren)." Are you kidding me!? This rationalisation comes predominantly from women which, I must hasten to clarify, is not intended to be a sexist slight in any way. It makes perfect sense given that the female bears the brunt of child-rearing across almost every animal species, humans included.

Speaking of the animal kingdom, I was recently watching a nature documentary which tracked a leopard as she went about day-to-day life in the African savannah. Soon after reaching maturity, she finds a mate (or rather the mate finds her). From there, she's pregnant and alone. This is normal, as leopards are solitary animals. She endures the full term of pregnancy and childbirth on her own, and then, in very much the same vein, we watch as she goes about rearing her two adorable little cubs alone. No midwives; no maternity leave; no husband/partner; no nanny or babysitter; no new mums' club to let off some steam, share ideas and trade sleepless-night-war-stories with other new mothers over a few glasses of wine. Just her, her new-born cubs, and the deadly daily perils of the wild.

From the day she gives birth until the day those cubs reach adolescence and leave her (if they haven't fallen victim to the numerous predators before then) she is focused primarily, and perhaps solely, on her cubs' survival. We follow her as she first has a run-in with hyenas and puts her life on the line to draw them away from her concealed cubs. She, and her cubs, come through that episode unscathed. But the hyenas have sensed that she has cubs, and they now know that she and those cubs are in the vicinity. After the dust settles and she has room to breathe, mother leopard must move her cubs. This is what she has to do every few days. After this encounter our mother leopard sets up den in the trees, out of the deadly reach of the hyenas and numerous other predators below. The life of this mother is not that simple though. Her cubs are safe from the dangers below, but she must remain equally vigilant. She is now very cognisant of a different, but equally lethal, threat – her species' eternal enemies that lurk in those very branches: baboons. Again, we're put through the suspense as she puts her life on the line to distract and do her best to fight off a troop of baboons, whilst simultaneously hoping that they don't sniff out and find her babies. This is now routine for this mother leopard, as it is across her species. Aside from a bit of luck, it is this mother's sheer determination and ferocity in the face of daily adversity, and nothing else, that stand between her cubs and their countless would-be killers.

In her spare time, when she's not fending off predators, mother leopard must go out and hunt to feed herself and, in time, her babies who can no longer be sustained on mother's milk alone. But each time she goes out hunting, she is resigned to the real possibility that she might return to find her babies gone. We, the emotionally invested viewers, know this just as well as we watch this suspense thriller dressed up as a nature documentary. On one such occasion, almost inevitably, that possibility comes to pass. Somewhat mercifully and miraculously, though, only one of her babies has been taken by whichever predator showed up on the day. The other cub remained safe and sound, palpably relieved to see mummy return. If I'm being honest, it was quite a tear-jerker, even for me who fancies himself as emotionally tough. Perhaps it was all exacerbated by the unbelievable cuteness of those leopard cubs!

It takes every ounce of this mother's guile, strength, determination and overall resolve to keep these cubs alive from day to day and see them through to adolescence. This daily "struggle" as we see it, is very much the norm in the life of every mother leopard and countless other species. It appears to be a struggle for us humans who watch the documentary while our children lie safely in their beds without a rabble of predators waiting at every corner. But to her, mother leopard, this was nothing out of the ordinary. This was life.

There are thousands, possibly millions, of video clips of similar incidents across various animal species. I have seen clips of a mother lion fighting off a crocodile to secure safe passage of her cubs across a river; a mother bear fighting off a rogue male almost twice her size, who was intent on killing her cubs and siring new ones of his own. It happens with domesticated animals too, like a mother hen defending her brood against the advances of a snake. Sometimes these brave fights are successful, but at least equally often, they are not. This is nature.

Back to our mother leopard. The daily struggles would continue until that surviving baby of hers reached adolescence and went off on her own. For the mother, it marked the end of one cycle. She would soon mate again, and commence a new, but identical cycle, riddled with the daily life-threatening occurrences that make up "normal life" in her world. And when she can longer reproduce, there is only one thing left for her. To wait for death. That is life in the animal kingdom. The purpose of life is to be the best parent possible and see your offspring safely to adolescence. And then do it all again (and again) until you die. But that is the animal kingdom, not the human world, and this hard-hitting reality should make us think about what we do with our lives and, equally important, what we could be and should be doing.

Human beings exist on a completely different plane to any other species. We are endowed with a super-computer brain, the capacity and power of which remain well beyond our own comprehension. We live in an age of limitless information available at the touch of a button (thanks, let's not forget, to the super-computer brains of those who came before us), from which we can garner all the knowledge we care to accumulate in pursuit of whatever we are trying to achieve. We have a duty to ourselves, our communities, our species and our Creator to do something worthwhile in this world. To leave a mark – a positive mark – that will long outlive ourselves and the children that we raise. The mark that you can make and leave on this world given your unique skillset, talents, interests and capabilities, and the act of working towards making that mark, is your purpose. In the life of the urban human being, being a parent is not, and cannot be, anyone's purpose.

In the same vein, I must burst the bubble of self-importance that many professionals inhabit; particularly the highly skilled, highly competent, highly experienced and, of course, highly paid professionals, principally those working for the biggest global corporations. There are of course exceptions to the rule. To *every* rule. The rule in the corporate world – the unspoken, inconvenient and uncomfortable rule that I now put to you – is that you are not making a difference to the world. Not in your personal capacity anyway. You are contributing something to a corporation. Perhaps most pertinently, you are contributing something to the bottom line of that corporation and, by extension, to the dividends that will line the pockets of that corporation's shareholders. There is nothing honourable or noble about your work. You are not leaving a legacy to this world. You're performing a specified role (one of dozens of roles within the corporation) and chances are you will not be remembered for it in the medium term let alone the long term. Certainly not by the world at large, and probably not even by that corporation that employed you. I once worked for a big corporate with a global behemoth as a shareholder. I headed the Human Capital department for a couple of years and oversaw at least two full scale staff re-structuring exercises. At every step of the way, the guiding principle was "we are not looking at people. We are looking at boxes on an organogram that need to be, and do not need to be, filled." This is the cold reality of corporate, which many people don't realise, or *won't* realise, because their ego and self-importance will not permit it. They will replace you when you leave and you will soon be forgotten as your replacement does an equally competent job and the bottom line remains healthy, or even grows. Or, worse, they will get rid of you when you have become surplus to requirements. If that's the path you choose, so be it. It's your life and your choice. Just don't bluff yourself into thinking you're doing anything purpose driven.

If you're a professional, you need to be doing something more than just efficiently making money for shareholders. You must be revolutionising your area in a way that will ultimately benefit people that you don't know and don't work for. A great example is Paul O Neill, a former CEO of Alcoa. While he oversaw a five-fold increase in turnover and a 200% increase in stock price during his tenure, he is not primarily remembered for that. His legacy, not only to Alcoa but to the world at large, is his revolutionary transformation of the way businesses looked at occupational health and safety.

Everyone is on a path of some sort. The path you're on, however, may not be (and probably isn't) your purpose. But it is also not a life sentence.

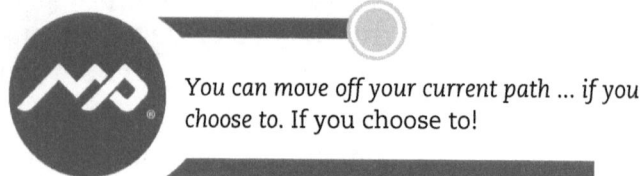

You can move off your current path ... if you choose to. If you choose to!

CHAPTER 18

IKIGAI

Ikigai, the Japanese concept which translates to "reason for being", provides a helpful outline for what one's purpose involves; a map of sorts if you like.

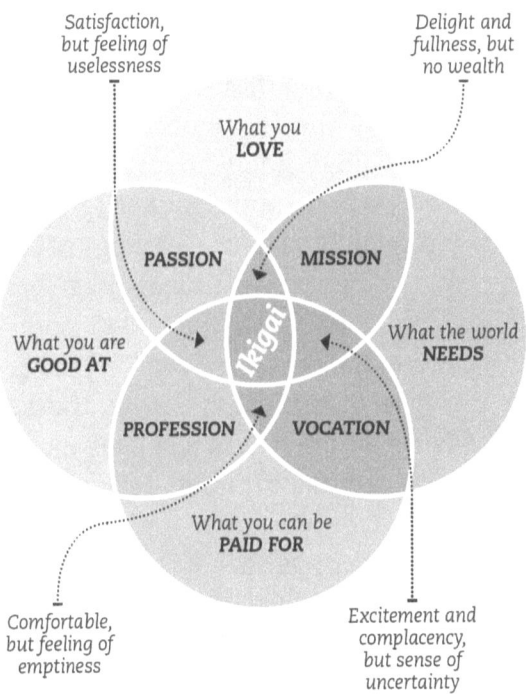

Figure 16.1: Ikigai – a Japanese concept meaning 'a reason for being'.
Source: Forbes.com – adapted from BodeTree and Francesc Miralles

In essence, Ikigai is doing something that ticks four critical boxes which are listed below, and depicted in Figure 16.1 above. They are:

- something that you love
- something that you're good at
- something that the world needs
- something that you can be paid for

One general shortcoming of the concept, at face value, is that it appears to focus on a person's career with one's family life conspicuous by its absence. This is easily explained though. My interpretation of the concept is that it is necessarily implied through 'something that you love'. For if your profession or your current occupation demands an inordinately high percentage of your time and consequently leaves you with less time than you would like for your family, you will soon stop loving what you are doing.

On the face of things, and with the consideration of family life that has just been explained, these four pillars make complete sense. But I have come to realise over the past four years since I first wrote about Ikigai, that each of these four pillars require closer individual examination. Beneath the surface lie questions. They are not obvious questions, but they are questions that must, nonetheless, be answered. Failure to identify and then answer these questions may well set you on a path towards the wrong destination.

Let's go through each of the four pillars more carefully.

DOING WHAT YOU LOVE

To what extent must one love what they do in order to tick this box? At face value it may seem obvious – either you love what you're doing, or you don't. It's a yes or no question, right? Wrong! There is a much broader meaning and extent than might meet the eye.

In the context of one's career, it extends far beyond simply doing the core job. There are other aspects – other unavoidable aspects – that are inseparably part of the package. From interacting with pushy and difficult co-workers to endless meetings that you know are completely unnecessary and serve only to eat away at the hours that you could be and should be spending doing those things that make up your core duties and that you love doing. And then there is the commute. Oh ... the commute!!!

Some fortunate people out there (myself included) continue, long after the pandemic landed its heaviest blows, to be beneficiaries of the Covid-induced work-from-home trend or innovation or whatever you like to call it. But the majority – the unfortunate majority – are well and truly back to the life of daily commuting.

I was in Zimbabwe on business, and that always entails a lot of driving. Exponentially more than my work-from-home norm. Thankfully it was for just a couple of weeks. Zimbabwe is a completely broken country. As much as it pains me deeply to say so, that is the sad reality. The economy is broken. The infrastructure is broken. There is no running water in large sections of major cities. Refuse is not collected. Ever! Households go 12 hours a day, every day, with no electricity. The unemployment rate is over 90%. Unbelievable and heart-breaking do not even begin to describe the situation. Amongst all of that, quite astonishingly, is a section of the population that goes to work every day in a manner that resembles what the world knows as normality. And to do so they must use a road network that has not been expanded for over 40 years, and that has barely been maintained at all over the same period. There are sections of road stretching dozens of metres that are riddled with potholes, many as wide as a car and half a foot deep. This is the same road network that was built, over four decades ago, for approximately 10% of the vehicles that currently burden it. Unbelievable is not the word!

I remember spending over an hour travelling a distance of less than 10km. To add to (and probably as the result of) everything else, the people are broken. And by that, I mean the moral fabric. This has become a population that simply does not care in the slightest about anything and anyone except themselves. They have been conditioned by everything else around them to simply do whatever they can do, and *must* do, to get themselves through another day. And then repeat the same thought pattern of survival tomorrow. What this means is that aside from the fragmented and grossly overpopulated road network and chaotic intersections that are the result of non-functioning traffic lights which, in turn, are the result of 12-hour daily power cuts, every motorist is now having to contend with a collection of hundreds of other motorists with zero courtesy or respect for the rules of the road. It is all broken!

So there I was. Stuck in the gridlocked traffic, contending with all these factors, as was every other motorist. I decided to conduct an informal social experiment if you like. I began to consciously and deliberately observe the facial expression of each motorist that drove past me in the opposite direction. And over the course of that hour there were well over a hundred. Every single one of them, without exception, looked like they were carrying the weight of the world on their shoulders as they painstakingly negotiated themselves through this traffic hell. In a sense, they all *did* have the weight of the world on their shoulders. It immediately struck me that these are very clearly stressed and unhappy people. But it also struck me that there must be a fair number of them that *do* love the jobs they do. The jobs from which they were returning home as I analysed their invariably haggard faces. And then it struck me further, if this is what a person has to go through every single day to get to their job and then to get home at the end of the day, would it be accurate to say that they love what they do? Part of that job that they do – a necessary part – is to actually get there to do the job, and then to get home when they're done for the day. For many people in Harare, that is an hour or more each way. Over two hours per day, which is over ten hours per week of traffic hell, not to mention the absolute hammering that all those cars take from what is left of the roads. How can a person love anything that necessarily incorporates those two hours of traffic hell every day?

A couple of months later I was in London. This time I was on holiday, so there was really no need for me to be commuting during rush hour. But I made the fatal mistake of losing track of time in the city, and before I knew it rush hour was upon me. I was caught in the thick of it, trying to get from central London out to Kent. As I negotiated my way through several underground stations, with platforms packed like sardines and commuters shoving like a seasoned pack of rugby forwards, I decided to perform a similar exercise to the one I had carried out in Harare. I began to observe the facial expressions of those around me. Those moving up and down the heaving escalators; those frantically rushing through crowded station concourses; those jostling for position on platforms long before their train arrived; and those occupying jam-packed train carriages. Unlike the Harare commuters, these people were not negotiating a broken road network and a broken society with no concern for the rules of the road of their fellow motorists. They were not battling, mentally, with a broken economy and broken infrastructure. In fact, these were commuters who have the daily benefit of a supremely efficient public transport system. Yet the facial expressions I witnessed mirrored those of their Harare counterparts, despite the vastly different conditions and circumstances. My journey, beginning from the time I walked into the first underground station in central London, took over an hour. No doubt other people's journeys took much longer. In fact, one of my closest friends who lives in greater London has previously complained about his daily two hour commute each way. I had no doubt that a fair amount of these grumpy, stressed and strained London commuters did like, perhaps even loved, their occupations. But the same question must be asked: How can a person love anything that necessarily incorporates that kind of stress and strain, both physical and mental, every day?

Throughout my professional life, going back to my first job, I hated Mondays. I was one of those that was highly susceptible to the amusing but brilliantly named Glenroe Fever. I still work a full-time job, but the Glenroe Fever is well and truly a thing of the past. I have been permanently cured! Monday could be any day in my work week. But how did I find the cure? It came about through this amazing, pandemic-induced concept called work-from-home. As I mentioned, for the past two years I've worked full time from home (with home being on a different continent to the office I worked in previously). The major difference? I don't commute. When Sunday evening comes, I'm completely at ease. There are things I no longer have to think about and stress about on Sunday evening nor, I know, will I have to when I wake up the following morning. Those stressors like running a few minutes late and the traffic jams that will catch me; wondering what I will wear and what I will have for lunch; remembering if I brought any files home on Friday that I must now take back in on Monday; checking if I have my laptop charger, and for that matter, checking if I have the laptop itself. Those thoughts and worries are all distant memories.

My wife is a teacher, and she likes – even loves – being a teacher. She has said as much herself. It may well be her purpose in life considering how she got there, through the force of life's nudges. She graduated with a master's degree in the history of art, with the intention of following that particular path and one day becoming the curator of an art museum. It didn't work out for one reason or another. To put it another way, life nudged her onto a different path. The teaching path. She really does love teaching and finds it particularly rewarding, as I'm sure anyone would, imparting knowledge and shaping so many young minds and lives year upon year. But (aside from the largely unavoidable daily commute) here's the catch – the actual *teaching* component is only one of many that the role demands. There is lesson preparation, grading and report writing. There are unavoidable dealings with overbearing parents who will simply not accept that little Johnny is not applying himself properly. No! His poor grades can only be attributable to poor teaching or a poor school system, or both. There are staff meetings that are invariably held after the long teaching day is over and there is little, if any, mental energy left in the tank. And then there are exams. Exams that must be set and invigilated, followed immediately by a very small window during which those exams must then be marked to form the basis for reports which must also be written. It doesn't end there. My wife doesn't particularly like many of those aspects of the job, and I doubt many teachers do. My wife likes *teaching*. But when you dig beneath the surface and look into it properly, you begin to see that the actual teaching component makes up little more than 50% of the job. Would it then be accurate for someone in that position to say, "I love what I do"? Digressing slightly, perhaps it's high time the job title of what we know as a teacher is changed to something that more accurately captures the full extent of the role.

I was much the same in my years as an

attorney. I enjoyed legal drafting and absolutely loved the excitement that litigating brought. The thrill of the court-room battle got the blood pumping like few other things could. And while the concept of purpose never crossed my mind, I thought I loved being a lawyer. As a naïve 23-year-old, I certainly revelled in the title and the attention at social gatherings when people found out I was a lawyer. It made me feel so important (yet that sense of importance makes me cringe now). But there was so much that I loathed: Regular visits to the dirty, dilapidated, disorganised, court registrars' offices to make follow ups; trips to the even more decrepit police stations when a client had been arrested – most commonly on trumped up price control violations in a broken economy; weekly credit meetings to explain why certain clients hadn't paid their legal fees timeously; subsequent calls to those very clients to awkwardly ask them why they had not paid their fees timeously; having to sit for over an hour in a baking, poorly ventilated, reeking courtroom until the presiding judge finally sauntered in, and then having to respectfully nod as he nonchalantly notified the court that his delay was due to some urgent matters that required attention on his farm; dealing with opposing lawyers who lacked any shred of ethics and scruples, and whose sole aim was to abuse the legal process and frustrate the other party for as long as possible. The things I hated about the job far outnumbered and outweighed the things I loved, or even liked. Yet, at the time, I was on that path and in my mind, it was the only path. I had successfully tricked myself into believing that I loved what I was doing. Until, thankfully, I got one of life's nudges – a necessarily strong one – that forced me off that path.

When you conclude that you love what you're doing, ensure that you have done so after a full and thorough examination and consideration of all the unavoidable secondary aspects of doing the primary thing that you do. You may well love what you primarily do. But you may also need to find a different way of doing it. A means and method of continuing to do what you love, but in such a way that you no longer have to do all that stuff you hate doing.

In one of my previous jobs I would from time to time go up to the finance department to follow up on certain things after getting no joy via email. There was one chap that stood out. His role was technical rather than managerial, so he was not bogged down by management meetings and so on. This was your typical number cruncher. I would marvel every time I went to the finance department as I looked at him, earphones in place, spreadsheets on his screen, and the most tranquil look on his face. I would have loved to know what music he was listening to, but I couldn't quite bring myself to disrupt the perfect serenity that he had created for himself. It was clear for the world to see; this guy loved what he was doing! And he had the pleasure and good fortune of being able to do what he loved for almost the entire workday.

SOMETHING YOU'RE GOOD AT

I have a 7-year-old daughter Emily, and a 4-year-old son, Dominic. On a regular basis I find myself having to deal with their sulking, pouting, even crying about not "being good" at certain things (or not being able to do them at all). From bouncing a basketball between their legs (as I do when I play with them) and shooting the basketball to riding a bicycle; from clicking their fingers to whistling; or just building Lego. It's a weekly thing. In Dominic's case, the reaction has been worsened by the fact that his older sister *can* now do things like whistle and click her fingers, so he feels like he has been left behind. Which he has, but don't tell him that.

My message is simple and largely unsympathetic (unlike their mother's) – nobody is born being good at anything. In another one of his masterpieces – Outliers – Malcolm Gladwell[36] puts it brilliantly: "We are so caught in the myths of the best and the brightest and the self-made that we think outliers spring naturally from the earth." In short, it all comes with practice. In some cases, it takes years and years of practice. At their young age my children appear to understand this on some level and, equally importantly, they accept it (at least for a few days until the next time they realise that they are not good at something that they probably never tried before).

The principle remains the same throughout life. You cannot just wake up one day being good at something, whether it is your purpose in life or not. I think we must all know this on some level, but it gets forgotten or overlooked in many instances. The way in which this concept, ikigai, is depicted is one such instance. It can easily elicit thoughts like "If it's my purpose, I must be good at it" or "If I'm not good at it, it can't be my purpose". Do we really think that we should, by some magical power, be instantly good at something purely because we have come to realise that it may well be our purpose? Nobody is born good at something. Nobody!

We have seen some prodigies in our time, particularly in sport. Golfer Tiger Woods[37] turned professional at age 20 and within less than 12 months he was the world number 1, a position he would hold for the vast majority of the following 13 years. Diego Maradona[38] became the youngest player to grace the top tier of Argentinean football when he debuted at the age of 15. Before he turned 24, he had become the world's most expensive player. Thrice! He would go on to almost single-handedly lead Argentina to world cup glory, and little-known Napoli Football Club to their first ever, and then their second Italian championships. The latter remains their last, more than three decades later. It's easy to conclude these two geniuses of their sports (and many others like them) had some supreme natural talent that few others had. Maybe they did. But let's look deeper.

Tiger Woods picked up a golf club at the age of one and began imitating his father's swing, just as every little boy imitates his father. By age three he was playing full rounds of golf on a regular basis, which he would continue doing throughout his childhood and beyond. Maradona received a soccer ball as a gift when he was three years old. From that day, he and that ball were literally inseparable. He would play with that ball from dawn until dark, and it became a running daily battle between young Diego and his mother to get him home at the end of each day. Even eating was not important to him. At the age of eight, he went for trials with a junior team and left the coach perplexed. It was evident to this coach that Maradona was a young boy but, according to that coach, he played soccer like an adult. It simply didn't make sense. He had never seen anything like it. It was the product of hours upon hour, day upon day for the preceding five years.

Innate talent or not, what we see is that the likes of Woods and Maradona were practising relentlessly from the age of three. Which 3-year-old child does that? Almost none. And therein lies the difference. Nobody, not even these prodigies of our time, is born good at anything. It is practice and dedication – day after day, week after week, month after month, and year after year – that set them apart from the rest.

Let's take a look at the greatest, most decorated Olympian the world has ever seen – Michael Phelps. He started swimming at the age of seven, which is quite late for any would-be professional swimmer. And the reason he started was not because he was good or appeared destined for greatness. Some accounts indicate that swimming was merely a way for him to "burn off some of the energy that was driving his mom and his teachers crazy".[39] After his retirement, Phelps himself recalled "the only reason I ever got in the water was my mom wanted me to just learn how to swim."[40] Whatever the truth behind the reason Phelps began swimming in the first place, one thing is clear: he didn't start swimming because he, or anyone else, thought he was or would be good at it, let alone the greatest. He would be spotted by a local swimming coach only much later. But again, it was not because he was good at swimming that he was noticed. He was *not* very good. He was noticed because that coach believed he could *become good* at swimming. The basis for that coach's belief, and the attributes that caught his attention, were not the way he swam, but rather his physique – his long torso, big hands and relatively short legs, meaning less drag.

What we see here is that even the greatest swimmer and greatest Olympian in human history, whose feats may never be surpassed, was not born "good". He couldn't even swim at the age of six. He had to work to become good. And then work harder to become even better. And then work even harder to become the best! The most important thing is that he started and didn't quit despite not being good at the onset.

Gladwell's *Outliers* carries an exposé of sorts that shows how the kids in various sporting disciplines that are deemed to be better than their peers, are actually not. What they are is older. He shows that in many sporting disciplines, the oldest kids *appear* to be better and more gifted but all they really are is that bit bigger and that bit stronger by virtue of being that bit older than those "less good". But what appears to be a "bit" older – 9 or 10 or 11 months – is massive in a class of 7 and 8-year-olds. An 11-month age difference can be a 13% age difference, which is huge. That is the equivalent of a 14-year-old competing against a 16-year-old. By virtue of being ostensibly better than their peers, these kids are selected for special training programmes and so on. By virtue of participating in these special training programmes with the extra hours and better coaching that come with them, these kids then *become* genuinely better than their peers. It is not by virtue of having been better at the onset and then simply maintaining the difference in inherent "good-ness".

Gladwell recounts a study carried out by Canadian Psychologist, Rodger Barnsley:[41]

> "Barnsley and his team gathered statistics on every player in the Ontario Junior Hockey League. More players were born in January than in any other month, and by an overwhelming margin. The second most frequent birth month? February. The third? March"

Barnsely then extended his analysis to the Canadian National Hockey League and, unsurprisingly, found that the number of players born between January and March was four times the number of those born between October and December.

The principle doesn't apply only to sports and physical activity. Gladwell moves on to the 10,000 hour rule, a concept originated by Swedish psychologist K. Anders Ericsson after a study at Berlin's Academy of Music. The rule says, in essence, that it takes 10,000 hours of practice in any field for a person to truly have mastered it and to become one of the best in the world. Over and above the Canadian hockey players and other sportsmen, Gladwell looks at various different disciplines, from music to technology. He carries out a fascinating exploration, among several others, of how Bill Gates came to found Microsoft.[42] How it was all a perfect storm that allowed young Bill Gates to spend thousands of hours on computer programming at a time when it was literally impossible for probably 99% of the world's population to do that.

> "In one seven-month period in 1971, Gates

> and his cohorts ran up 1,575 hours of computer time on the Information Sciences Inc. mainframe, which averages out to eight hours a day, seven days a week."

The point was not to detract from Gates' achievements in any way. Rather to show how he was able to, and did, get in the magic 10,000 hours in the computer programming world before practically everyone else. Regarding Ericsson's study, Gladwell shares this insight:[43]

> "The striking thing about Ericsson's study is that he and his colleagues couldn't find any 'naturals'; any musicians who floated effortlessly to the top while practising a fraction of the time their peers did. Nor could they find any 'grinds', people who worked harder than anyone else, yet just didn't have what it takes to break the top ranks."

The overarching point here is that you need to *become* good at anything you do – whether you are innately more talented than others or not; whether you have better opportunities or not; and, most importantly in the context of this chapter and this book, whether you think it is your purpose or not. And to become good takes a lot of time, effort and dedication. Don't fool yourself into thinking there is some magical, prodigious talent you need to unearth within yourself which will then have the effect of miraculously propelling you to success in that field. To take another quote from Gladwell:

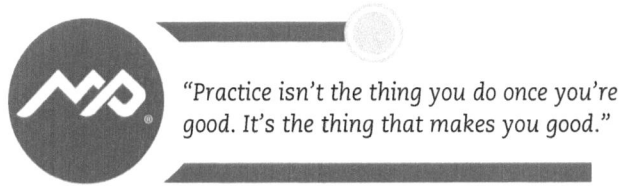

"Practice isn't the thing you do once you're good. It's the thing that makes you good."

There is no doubt in my mind that I have found my purpose in life – writing. This is my fourth book. Whether I am actually good at writing or not is something I don't know. And to be honest, it doesn't really matter to me. What I *do* know is that my writing is better now than it was when I wrote my first book. And I have every reason to believe that when I write my fifth, sixth and seventh books, the standard of writing will be better than it is now. That is what happens when you keep practising and keep doing something. How could I not take the very advice that I give to my children on a weekly basis?

One of life's great mysteries is the way children, with their limited capacity for understanding, easily and quickly grasp the fact that they will fail at first, but they must pick themselves up and carry on. Which they do. From learning to walk, to riding a bicycle or doing their sums and spelling. Adults however, with their superior intelligence and reasoning capacity, are the opposite. You find adults who take their first piano lesson or play their first round on the golf course, and then vow never to do it again, because "I'm not good at it." The principal applies to so many activities, from painting or public speaking to opening a small business. "I'm not good at it" may well be the obstacle that is preventing you from finding your purpose.

If it is something you enjoy doing, start doing it. Start dedicating more time to it, and as you do, you will become better at it. That is simple logic. Don't allow yourself to overthink and over-complicate it.

SOMETHING THE WORLD NEEDS

"The world" is a big place; a broad concept; and a daunting prospect. Just like the "requirement" to be good at something, it can be so overwhelming that it becomes off-putting and downright scary. The typical thought process would be something like "Can I – little old me – really do something that extends to the whole world?" Under such circumstances, the default setting is to cast aside those intimidating thoughts and go with the safer, easier, less daunting option. The comfort zone looks far more appealing.

"The world" doesn't have to, and shouldn't, be interpreted literally. Start with your community. After all, the world is made up of a collection of communities. Do something that is worthwhile to the community at large, because when you do that, you are impacting the world. Do something that leaves a legacy. Do something that will be remembered after you're gone. Like I said in the previous chapter, most professions as we know them do not, unfortunately, fulfil this. And, dare I say, those "successful" professionals who would like to argue otherwise are regrettably caught in a web of misplaced self-importance.

I look back on my own professional career and in particular my years as an attorney. Putting aside the aspects of the job that I didn't like, I had a flair for litigation and legal drafting, and became better at it with each passing year. But what was I really doing for the community? For the world? The answer is – nothing! I was putting in the hours, billing the client and moving on to the next file. When I left that job, I received calls from a few clients asking why I had left and where they could find me. They told me how they liked the way I had handled their cases over the years, and they still wanted me to do their work. Needless to say, it made me feel good. It made me feel important. But I told them that I had moved into corporate and could no longer do work for external clients. In some instances, I would meet for lunch with clients that I had built very strong relationships with and we would talk about issues they were dealing with and I'd offer informal advice where I could. Within a year or two it all but fizzled away. They had found different lawyers, no doubt equally or more competent than I was, to take care of them. I was good at what I did, but there were dozens, possibly hundreds, of equally competent lawyers in Harare. I had not made any special mark on the world. I had just done my job competently. Nothing more, nothing less.

I moved into the corporate sector, where I've been for 15 years. Again, I've become better at my job with every passing year but what am I really contributing to the community and to the world? Nothing! I do my job, get paid a fixed salary each month, rinse and repeat. Over those 15 years in corporate I've worked for four different companies, including my current employer. The previous three replaced me soon after I left and likely forgot about me soon after. That says nothing about me – whether good or bad. It's just the way the corporate world works. There was nothing important about me in any of those jobs. I was just filling a box in a staff organogram. And that's what most jobs are, regardless of job title, the salary or the perceived level of importance. They are just boxes on an organogram, which can quickly be (and often are) filled by any one of hundreds of suitably qualified people out there.

This has been the stark reality of my professional life to date. And for me to believe anything else, as much as it might inflate my ego, would be to create and believe false hype about myself. There is nothing good about being caught up in that web of misplaced self-importance.

A professional who wants to make a difference in the world needs to do something different; something better. Something that is not the routine expectation of any other competent person in the same profession. Like Paul O Neill at Alcoa, whom we spoke about in chapter 17. In the realm of my own profession, a lawyer who wants to make a difference to the world can't just put in the billable hours and move on. There is nothing exceptional about that. Any and every lawyer in private practice does that. And the thing about the legal profession is that lawyers bill according to time spent on the work, rather than the output. So even if the case is lost (and even if the lawyer was largely incompetent), he is still happily billing his client and, more happily, getting paid. In many respects it is quite ludicrous. If the legal (or other) profession is your purpose, you need to be doing something exceptional. Do more *pro bono* work that meaningfully impacts the section of society that routinely has their legal rights flouted and abused, but who cannot financially afford to assert and protect their rights. Become a Member of Parliament, with a view *not* to garnering as many benefits as you can, but to changing antiquated and oppressive legislation. Become a human rights or environmental lawyer. The world needs more of those.

Or don't. But when you choose to sit in your plush office, in any profession, and do largely routine work and enjoy the significant financial rewards, don't fool yourself into thinking that you're making a difference in the world. You're performing a profession, not living your purpose. Know the distinction and make the distinction.

Every person can have a direct impact on bettering the world, by merely bettering their community.

WHAT YOU CAN BE PAID FOR.

Lo and behold, we're back to money! The need to be paid for what you do, and its explicit inclusion as one of the pillars of a person's reason for being, makes sense on the face of things. It is consistent with what I have said on numerous occasions previously – money is necessary to meet our daily needs, ideally with some level of comfort. To think otherwise is idealistic and folly. Beneath the surface, however, there is scope to be not only misled, but restricted and discouraged in the pursuit of one's purpose.

What this pillar does is provide a very strong suggestion, or even stipulation, that pursuing your purpose must, itself, generate the income you require to live. To reiterate, everyone does require monetary income to live. And if it can and does arise through your purpose, that represents an ideal situation. *The* ideal situation. The first prize, as it were. But what if it doesn't, then what? Does that mean you must discard that particular activity? Does the failure to tick this box preclude that activity from being your purpose? The answer would appear to be yes if the concept of ikigai is taken at face value. I've only recently come to realise that, much to my own personal relief, this is not the only way.

I came to the realisation that writing was my purpose in life about five years ago. In that time I've written and published three books. To date, they are largely unsuccessful in financial terms. That comes as no surprise given the fact that I've done very little in the way of marketing. I've kept my day job, because I have financial commitments which my three published books cannot yet meet. I always told myself that I would have to keep my day job and in my free time do whatever I could in the way of marketing my books (over and above writing new ones) so that I would eventually be in the position where my book sales were generating enough income to meet the financial obligations that life throws my way. When that happened, and *only* when that happened, I would be in a position to quit my job to properly and fully live out my purpose. But the reality is that a day job allows little time and scope to write new books *and* to effectively market existing ones. In any event, I really don't like marketing and all that it entails!

I had become trapped for years in this erroneous and limiting mindset. The worst of it all was that it was all weighing on my mind. I would frequently and anxiously ask myself whether I would ever generate sufficient book sales. That wasn't because I doubted the saleability of my books and the value in their content. It was because I knew that marketing those books – whether I like it or not – is essential to selling them. People cannot buy a product if they don't know that the product even exists, regardless of how good the product might be. And I knew that I had very little time in my schedule; even less know-how; and *even* less desire to do that marketing. The end result was lingering stress and, of course, a lower Happiness Score. In my case, marketing my books is one of those undesirable secondary aspects of the primary thing I love to do. I had to, and I did, find a different way of doing it that eliminated that unwanted aspect.

I have found a cheat code, if you like, that everyone can use. While money is necessary, it need not necessarily come from the activity of living out your purpose. This is perhaps the greatest value of passive income. I no longer need to worry about marketing and selling books; and stressing myself because my books are not selling. I shall carry on with my day job, but not for the reasons I previously thought were compelling me to do so. I shall save money that I earn through my day-job and look for investment opportunities; investments that will give me adequate passive income to meet the needs of myself and my family. And when my passive income reaches an acceptable level, I will be free to fully and properly live out and enjoy my purpose as a full-time writer, without a care in the world about how many books I will sell. I don't need my books to be financially successful in my lifetime. I just need to know that the people who read them, as modest as the numbers may be, are positively impacted by them. And that my books will remain my legacy to this world long after I'm gone.

The act of living your purpose doesn't necessarily have to generate the income you need.

Find something you love doing; something that makes you feel good just by doing it. When that happens, becoming good at it will be an unavoidable biproduct. Then find a way of making a difference to the world, starting with your community. If you can earn a decent living from it all, great. If not, don't be deterred. There is a thing called passive income, which will financially allow you to actively pursue your purpose.

PART VI
CONCLUSION

CHAPTER 19

SUCCESS AND HAPPINESS: JOINED AT THE HIP

> "I was successful but miserable."

And so, we find ourselves having come full circle. Back to where we began, with the very statement that sparked a seemingly simple question: "Is it possible to be 'successful but miserable?" This seemingly simple question which has, somehow, grown and transformed itself into a book.

By now we should have the unequivocal answer to the question. A resounding *no*, in case you were still unclear. We should now also be able to identify what this statement is, so often, intended to mean. It's expanded meaning, if you like:

> "I was *financially* successful, but miserable."

While this expansion makes the statement more accurate and certainly easier to identify with, it presents a misleading implication and, in turn, a limiting and restrictive mindset. The automatic and largely unconscious inference that the terms "successful" and "financially successful" can be used inter-changeably represents an erroneous simplification that can be costly to our pursuit of *real* success. We must be equipped to identify this popularisation for the fallacy that it is. For there are so many different aspects to success, financial success being only one. In the grander scheme of life, only one *small* aspect.

The statement can be expanded further to give even more accuracy:

> "I was successful in my career, but miserable in life on the whole."

Let's park that thought for a minute, as I ask that you picture yourself hosting a Christmas dinner. You've gone with a traditional menu of stuffed turkey, roast potatoes and Brussel sprouts. But for one reason or another, things have managed to go horribly wrong. You surely wouldn't sit down to dinner and announce to your guests "I successfully made the perfect Brussel sprouts, but the turkey and potatoes are burnt, and the stuffing is bone-dry." It wouldn't even cross your mind! What you would, almost certainly, think to yourself is that the meal is a disaster. For their part your guests may, out of a combination of awkwardness, sympathy and good manners, end up complimenting you on the delightful Brussel sprouts as they remain mum on the patently disastrous other aspects of the meal. But you will know the reality. You will know that, regardless of those impeccable Brussel sprouts, they can see your meal for the overall failure that it is, just as clearly as you can. The accurate description is that the meal is unsuccessful (and miserable).

Ultimately, this thing we are all acting out during our time on earth is *life as a whole*. There are various different components, but they all come together in one way or another to give a certain quality of life. They cannot be looked at in isolation, which is precisely what so many people do with their careers and the money that those careers bring. Life, in many respects, is like that Christmas dinner. Your career (and how much money you have) is but one of the many components that make up your life. It is those successfully cooked Brussel sprouts in the midst of your Christmas dinner. The question, to repeat, is not how successful the Brussel sprouts are, but "what is the overall quality of the meal?" What is the overall quality of your life?

Just like your guests at the Christmas dinner, those around you can see the shortcomings and misery in various aspects of your life but will be loath to say anything. They will probably feel, and perhaps rightly so, that it is not their place. They will choose instead to comment on the positives – those perfectly prepared Brussel sprouts – that they see, whether it be out of awkwardness, nervous uncertainty, sympathy or something else.

Don't expect more from others; demand more of yourself instead. The important thing is for *you* to see things as they are. Don't hide behind your Brussel sprouts and say you are successful (but miserable). Identify the misery and its source, and then do something about it.

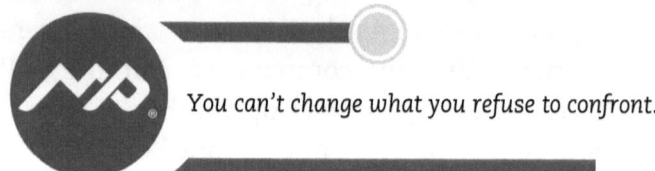

You can't change what you refuse to confront.

If the successes of individual aspects of life are adding up to an overall positive living experience (the Happiness Score), then happy days. Literally! There is success all round. If the "success" of certain aspects of life is coming at the cost of misery in other aspects – other *important* aspects – then there is no overarching success. There is overarching misery. In the grander scheme of life, you are miserable. Not "successful but miserable", just miserable! You see, they are mutually exclusive terms. They are winning and losing. Winning *at life* or losing *at life*. You cannot be doing both simultaneously.

Success and happiness, on the other hand, are the best of friends. They are like "q" and "u". I often tell my children that "q" has a best friend, and her name is "u". That they are such good friends that you will never find the letter "q" in any word if her best friend is not there next to her. That is success and happiness. You will not find success where there is no happiness. It might be something else dressed up as success, but it is not success. They are mutually inclusive. To use a term that takes me back to my Criminal Law lectures 20 years ago, happiness is the *sine qua-non* for success. They are joined at the hip! Like we established in chapter 16 the best way to measure success is, quite simply, by how happy you are. And that, in turn, is the Happiness Score.

CHAPTER 20

BRINGING IT ALL TOGETHER

- Successful but miserable! A state that on the face of things seems not only possible, but quite common. I put it to you that it cannot exist. At the very least, it should elicit certain questions that must be seriously considered by all of us: Doesn't the notion of success necessarily exclude scope for misery? Can success and misery co-exist in the same person or are they mutually exclusive? Isn't happiness a core component of success? Or shouldn't it be? And, if so, how does this happiness exist in an environment of misery? Surely it cannot?

- We appear to all have fallen on some level into the Trap. We focus primarily on financial success, not just assuming, but *expecting*, that happiness will automatically follow as the inevitable consequence of having attained financial success. Life doesn't work that way, unfortunately. Or is it fortunately? While you're focusing so diligently on attaining financial success, the rest of your life – the good things; the things that *do* make you happy – are passing you by. That is the Trap. Get out of it!

- Make a gratitude list. Put aside the concept of success and in particular financial success and think about what happiness means to you. What is important in your life? You'll probably find that the answer lies, to a large extent, in what you already have as opposed to the money (and the things it can buy) that you are mindlessly chasing. What are you grateful for? The answer to that question goes a long way towards answering "What is important to me?" Enjoy and cherish those things while you have them. Focus on those things rather than casting them aside and taking them for granted in the name of chasing more money. When you do that you will force yourself to become consciously aware of, and thankful for, what you do have rather than beating yourself up about what you don't have.

- We live in an age where there is a compulsion to measure. This goes a long way to explaining this propensity we have to fall into the Trap. You see, money is easily measured and provides an easy proxy for success and happiness. Success – and I mean *success* in the broad sense as opposed to the restrictive *financial success* that probably springs to mind – and happiness can be measured in non-monetary terms. I call it the Happiness Score, and it has a simple formula that gives a numerically quantifiable value. Your happiness score is the proportion of time spent in your day; your week; your month in a state of contentment. A state that excludes negative emotions.

- Life is riddled with stress triggers – both external, like someone cutting in front of you in rush hour traffic; or internal like the jealousy we feel when we see other people flaunting their material things and their "success". Whether internal or external, these triggers represent only potential stress. Whether we then become stressed or not – whether we *allow ourselves* to become stressed or not – is within our control. We can choose not to allow certain triggers to stress us and, in so doing, increase our happiness score. We can, quite simply, choose to make ourselves happier.

- Confusing happiness and pleasure, or lumping them together as one and the same thing, is one of the biggest obstacles standing between you and *real* happiness. There is a difference between happiness and pleasure. When you make that distinction, you take a giant step in the direction of happiness and away from a life of chasing short-lived pleasures on the erroneous assumption that more pleasure equals more happiness. It does not! The distinction is backed by science. The feeling of happiness is experienced through the release of serotonin while pleasure, on the other hand, is triggered by dopamine. One of the most convincing distinctions however, and one that is easy to notice by considering our own experiences, is that happiness can only exist in a state of safety while pleasure is equally at home in a state of safety or threat. Perhaps the most critical distinguishing factor is internal versus external. Happiness comes from within; from the state of affairs existing in your life at a given time and from your baseline reality. It is your day-to-day norm, or your default setting. Pleasure, by contrast, comes from external sources that we go looking for, often in a bid to improve our day-to-day norm.

By all means treat yourself to some of life's pleasures from time to time. They are as necessary as they are pleasing, for they serve to take the edge off the oft monotonous and draining obligations that life throws up. The trick is *not* to allow those pleasures to become compulsive and addictive; and, most importantly, to make sure not to confuse them for happiness.

- Nostalgia is a special, magical feeling. It can be triggered by any number of things from music, photographs and smells; to re-visiting places or buying that pair of shoes that you wished you had as a teenager. They all have the effect of mentally transporting you back in time. More specifically, to a happy time that can be re-lived mentally. Look for those triggers and soak up the nostalgia when you get the opportunity. It will do wonders for your soul and for your Happiness Score.

- Closely related to the distinction between happiness and pleasure; and equally important, is the distinction between needs and desires. Our needs must be met in order for us to have any decent quality of life, or life at all! This is the non-negotiable foundation upon which happiness is built. Desires are different. They are not necessary for happiness, and they often take the form of materialistic things that we generally cannot afford; designer clothes, performance cars and so on. We end up inviting so much stress upon ourselves because of the desires that we cannot satisfy, that we forget to be thankful for and enjoy all the positives in our lives. If you can only reconfigure your mindset to the reality that nobody worthwhile actually cares about your material possessions, you will become a lot more content. A lot happier. And that is the reality. Nobody worthwhile cares about your material possessions. This is consistent with Socrates' philosophy:

> "The secret of happiness, you see, is not found in seeking more but in developing the capacity to enjoy less".

- Focus on impressing yourself, rather than strangers. Do the things that make you feel good about yourself. Buy clothes that make you look in the mirror and think "I look good", not merely because there is an expensive brand name across the chest, and not because you think it will impress strangers. When you master the art of not caring about the opinions of people that carry no relevance in your life you become mentally liberated, less stressed and your Happiness Score goes up. And when you succeed in impressing yourself, your self-confidence improves. You reduce, and hopefully eliminate, the stress associated with negative self-image. This means an increased Happiness Score.

- In a way, life is the sum of our relationships. The thing about relationships, though, is that they all need to be nurtured and nourished in order to stay healthy. That requires time. When we don't dedicate enough time to a particular relationship, it will fade away and eventually die, often leaving us with regret. Make a deliberate effort to nurture the relationships that matter before it's too late, because the active relationships we have, and those we should have but do not, directly impact our happiness.

- Money is not inherently bad or evil. But money needs to be looked at with a clear and objective mind rather than the mindless manner in which we have been conditioned – whether consciously or subconsciously – to not only view, but even worship, it. There is no doubt that money is necessary to meet our needs. And meeting our needs is the minimum requirement and the foundation upon which happiness must be built. Beyond meeting our needs, however, the value and the very nature of money takes a sinister turn, and it is important to be cognisant of it.

- From time to time we all scrutinise that sequence of digits on a piece of paper, or a computer or phone screen, which purport to represent our bank or investment portfolio balance. More importantly, we consider what that sequence of numbers means to our lives. But how do we know that those digits do actually represent what we have? We have seen countless instances of money disappearing literally overnight. One of the most widely reported examples was the

Bernie Madoff scam. $60 billion worth of investments, for which statements were sent out religiously to investors. Suddenly, and almost overnight, there was no money. Those investments were gone. We have seen equally frequent reports of governments and central banks creating money out of thin air. They call these creations "liquidity injections" and other fancy names that carry no real explanation into what has actually happened. But put aside these news stories, and the technical complications of what governments and central banks do at will, one thing we all know for certain is that we cannot walk into a bank and withdraw any significant amount of money – our own money as represented on our bank statements – in the form of cash. Cash is what turns illusion into reality in the world of money. Why can't we get all our money in cash? Because it doesn't really exist! It is an illusion.

- Our minds and mindsets have been attuned and conditioned over generations to see money as the cost to be paid for almost everything in life. But what about the cost of earning or acquiring that money? There _is_ a cost, and it comes in the form of our time; our relationships; our dreams; and our health. In short, the act of chasing money often comes at the cost of our happiness. And this is the crux of one of life's great paradoxes. While we go out chasing more money, on the blind and foolish assumption that it will bring with it more happiness, that very act – the act of chasing more money – is slowly but surely costing us our happiness!

- Are you selling your soul to the devil? Your soul is represented by your dreams, your purpose and your over-all happiness. The devil is represented by money (and the pleasures that money buys). What is the cost you are paying for your money? To what extent are you selling your soul to the devil? Is it worth it?

- A natural aspect of human nature is to worry. Some people worry more than others, but we all do it. What we all also do, to varying degrees, is worry about things *that may never happen*. These often endless "what ifs". What if I fall seriously ill, what if I lose my job, and so on? The list can be endless. Money – in its illusory form – provides the answer to these often equally illusory *what ifs*. Money allows us to cast them aside, and with them the associated fear, anxiety and other negative emotions that routinely reduce our Happiness Score. In short, money can provide something non-material but priceless if viewed correctly – peace of mind.

- Success is a very broad concept, and one of

the things that cannot be overemphasised is that *financial* success is merely one small component of it. Success, as I see it, takes two distinct but equally important forms. The first is what I call ultimate success which, in essence, is living out your purpose in life. There can be no greater success than that. The second is what I call day-to-day success which is, essentially, achieving the goals we set for ourselves. This is conditional though. It is conditional upon those goals actually making us happy. If we achieve goal after goal; day after day but are not any happier for them, then that is something other than success. It's ticking boxes for the sake of ticking boxes. This brings us back to happiness. It may seem idealistic and simplistic at first glance (it certainly did to me, and I said as much in my first book back in 2019) but success is measured by how happy you are. That measure encompasses all aspects of life – including, but not limited to, financial success. The major problem with such a measure would be trying to put a numerical value to it. We now have exactly that in the form of the Happiness Score and its formula.

- Purpose – or life purpose – is something powerful and compelling. It is not a destination, but rather an ongoing, fantastic, fulfilling, rewarding and gratifying journey. It is different from a path. Everyone is on a path – *some* path – at any given moment. It can be a path to somewhere or something good, or quite the opposite. To find one's purpose in life often entails stepping off the path you're on which, in turn, often means stepping out of our comfort zone. This is not a once off, but rather something that happens several times over through the course of our lives. But we find that difficult. We often find it *too* difficult. It entails change, to which human beings are inherently averse. This is why, throughout our lives, we experience what I call Life's Nudges. These are necessary pushes, often disguised as problems and obstacles, that get us off our current path and onto a new and better one. One that is more likely to lead to our purpose. Purpose is something more than a job or a profession or being a good parent. We are built for more. Much more! Purpose is something that leaves its mark on this world – whether globally or just the community that you live in – but a mark, nonetheless, that will long outlive yourself.

- The Japanese concept of Ikigai (translated to "reason for being") provides a good guideline to finding one's purpose. It has four pillars – what you love doing; what you're good at; what the world needs; and what you can be paid for. It should be emphasised, however, that this provides a good *guideline* for purpose, as opposed to a rulebook. Each of the four pillars must be examined in detail in the specific context of each person's own circumstances.

- "What you love doing", in the context of one's occupation may seem like a straightforward consideration with an equally straightforward yes or no answer. It is quite the opposite. There are aspects – perhaps secondary aspects but recurring ones nonetheless – of every person's occupation that they do not like. That they even loathe. When you conclude that you love what you're doing, ensure that you have done so after a full and thorough examination and consideration of all the unavoidable secondary aspects of doing the primary thing that you do. You may well love what you primarily do. But you may also need to find a different way of doing it; a means and method of continuing to do what you love, but in such a way that you no longer have to do all that stuff you hate doing.

- "Something you're good at" can be misleading and, worse, has the propensity to be off-putting. The apparent implication, which is an erroneous one, is that someone must be inherently good at something for it to qualify as one's purpose. Nobody is born good at anything. Not even the "prodigies" of our time. "Being good" at something is something *to become*, rather than something that you *just are*. It is the product of dedication and persistence. As Malcolm Gladwell most aptly puts it, "Practice isn't the thing you do once you're good. It's the thing that makes you good." If it is something you enjoy doing, start doing it. Start dedicating more time to it, and as you do, you will inevitably become better at it.

- "Something the world needs" is, again, somewhat misleading. "The world" is a big place, a broad concept and daunting prospect. It doesn't have to, and shouldn't, be interpreted literally. Start with your community. If you're doing something that objectively benefits your community and will leave a positive mark on it long after you're gone, you're well on your way to living your purpose.

- "What you can be paid for" is easy to understand but can be daunting as well. It creates a burden. It generates fear and holds us back from leaving the financial safety net of the job we hate. It elicits thoughts like "what if my project fails?" After all, we all need money to meet our needs, whether we like it or not. That is the baseline requirement for happiness. But there is a cheat code. Start looking into investments that generate passive income. If you can generate sufficient passive income, it eliminates the need for your purpose-driven venture to immediately meet your financial needs, and you can freely go about it without that burden weighing you down.

- Find something you love doing. Something that makes you feel good just by doing it. When that happens, becoming good at it will be an unavoidable biproduct. Then find a way of making a difference to the world, starting with your community. If you can earn a decent living from it all, great. If not, don't be deterred. There is a thing called passive income, which will financially allow you to actively pursue your purpose.

- Life is made up of a whole host of different components that come together to give an overall quality of life. Financial success is merely one aspect of life, and it shouldn't serve as the rug under which all other miserable aspects can be swept. If the successes of individual aspects of life are adding up to an overall positive living experience (the Happiness Score), then there is success all round. But if the success of certain aspects of life are negatively impacting other aspects – other *important* aspects – then there is a problem. There is no overarching success. It is far more likely that there is overarching misery. In the grander scheme of life, you are not "successful but miserable", just miserable! You see, they are mutually exclusive terms. They are winning and losing. Winning *at life* or losing *at life*. You cannot be doing both simultaneously.

- In the end, happiness and success are inseparable. They are mutually inclusive terms. "Successful but miserable" is a mythical creature that cannot exist in reality. The happier you are and the higher your Happiness Score, the more successful you are.

APPENDIX A

THE DIFFERENT SHADES OF YOU

In Part 3 of this book, we'll unpack the specific shades of you, what they entail, how they play out in reality, and how they interact and overlap with other shades. It makes sense, then, to start by unpacking some of these shades and providing some relatable examples as a reference point for the remainder of the book.

Some of these shades exist in all people, while others are more unique to certain individuals. And it's important to appreciate that this is not a closed list. The onus is on you to do a bit of self-introspection and to consider your own unique set of circumstances and the unique shades of yourself. Bear in mind that there are several overlaps across various shades, which we will look at as we unpack the different shades in more detail.

- *You, the child*

This is, perhaps, the most appropriate starting point because this is how every life began. Every person entered the world as someone's child, and the majority of us set off on this journey of life possessing this shade. There are many adults – perhaps the fortunate ones – who are still children to someone.

This shade of you captures the relationship you have with your parent(s) or those who raised and cared for you, and everything that goes into that relationship.

- *You, the physiological being*

The irony is that this is the single-most important, yet also easily the most neglected shade. For many people, this is an aspect of life that is routinely taken for granted and which seldom gets any conscious acknowledgement at all. In a nutshell, every person is a physiological being. There are certain things that we all *need* in order to merely stay alive. This includes air, water, food, sleep and other things. And whatever you do to get these essentials is being done in your capacity as a physiological being.

- *You, the sibling*

Your siblings are your first friends. They know and understand you better than anyone else, and the same goes for your understanding of them. They know secrets of yours that no one else does. They're the only people with whom you can have a good heart-to-heart chat about certain things, including, for example, the way your ageing parents are behaving! This is a hugely important and unique relationship, yet it is one that often gets neglected, or bundled up with other shades. Be careful not to neglect these very special relationships, this very special shade of yourself.

- *You, the grandchild*

This shade does not apply to the vast majority of people. While growing up I, along with my sister, fell into the minority: *you, the grandchild* was one of the shades that applied to me. Our paternal grandparents were everything to my sister and me. With our parents having divorced before I can even remember, my grandparents provided a sense of stability and normality. While my father had his house, and my mother had hers, the place that felt most like home was always my grandparents' house. They were grandparents in the conventional sense, spoiling us, etc. but they were also parents in many senses. And to add to it all, I always called my grandfather "my best friend".

My grandmother passed away when I was 19. I'm convinced that the timing is no coincidence. She safely and necessarily guided and nurtured me through my childhood and teenage years, and could then go in peace. My grandfather lived on for almost another 20 years, well into his nineties. And well into my adult life.

The point, really, is to demonstrate that we all have our own shades that may not, on the face of things, be apparent to us, let alone to others.

For almost all of my adult life to date, I was my grandfather's grandson, which was a shade of me, separate and distinct from every other. Visiting my grandfather was not the same as visiting my father or my mother. I needed to treat this shade as a stand-alone aspect of my life and give it the attention it warranted and deserved.

- *You, the parent*

The things that immediately come to mind here are paying school fees, feeding your children (literally spoon-feeding them, as well as ensuring that there is food in the house), watching their sports matches and concerts, helping them with their homework, and so on. But the love and concern that is evoked by becoming a parent can consume a person almost entirely. It goes far beyond just these common activities and financial obligations, and we'll explore this in Chapter 5.

- *You, the friend*

This is, perhaps, a bit tricky in that it is sometimes difficult to determine if you are acting in your own or your friend's interests. As with any relationship, it's a two-way thing. The relationship must present clear benefits to both you and your friend. Which then raises the question … "Am I doing things for my own benefit, or am I doing things for my friend's benefit?" The answer is both. The things you do as a friend will either be more beneficial to you, more beneficial to your friend, or of equal benefit to you both.

Where you are doing something more for the benefit of your friend than for yourself, then you are acting almost entirely in your capacity as *you, the friend*. An easily identifiable example is helping your mate move house.

If you are doing something that is more beneficial to you – for example going to your friend's fortieth birthday party, which you've been looking forward to so much for the past two months, then you're really acting more in your capacity as *you, just you*, which is summarised a few points below. But your friend will also be glad that you came, so there is an overlap. Activities like this, which present overlaps, are great. Because you are essentially killing two birds (two shades of yourself) with one stone (one pocket of time).

- *You, the spouse*

If you are married, or have a significant other, your relationship with your partner comes with certain expectations and obligations which are unique. What is very important yet often overlooked, however, is the distinction between *you, the spouse* and *you, the parent*. The distinction is often clouded to the extent that it is rendered non-existent. We'll look at that more.

- *You, the employee*

On the face of things, this is perhaps the most obvious shade of life. Yet, to a large extent, it is debatable as to whether or not it is actually a stand-alone shade. We'll look at this more in Part 4, and ultimately you can decide for yourself. Either way, if you have a formal job, then you get up and go to work every day, perform your duties, and go home. Which makes *you, the employee*, arguably the most easily identifiable and easily segregated aspect of your life. For now, we'll treat it as a shade of you.

- *You, the dreamer*

I believe that there was, at some point, a dreamer in everyone. And, if it hasn't come to the fore, it is still there, somewhere, capable of being discovered. What varies from person to person is the type and magnitude of the dream and, most critically, what plans and actions you are putting in place towards making that dream a reality. Buried and suppressed dreams will play on your subconscious mind without you knowing it, and you'll wonder why you have this constant feeling of a lack of fulfilment, and of regret. This is a specific shade that everyone needs to pay attention to.

- *You, the spiritual being*

This may present a bit of controversy (which is not necessarily a bad thing), and I suppose it is far more a matter of opinion than fact.

There are countless definitions of "spirituality", and I won't attempt to unpack or critique them.

My view, in a nutshell, is that spirituality refers to a connection to something bigger than mere human existence and interaction. It is aimed at nurturing the soul.

I am firmly of the opinion that this shade of life, more than any other, is what distinguishes us, human beings, from animals and, indeed, machines. As we enter the age of artificial intelligence, one could easily argue that machines now, for all intents and purposes, have brains. Brains that are, in many respects, superior to ours. But what they do not have, and will never have, is a soul. Regardless of what you believe will happen to your soul after death, as long as you are alive on this earth, you have a soul. And that soul needs to be nurtured to complete you and fulfil you.

Some people attend traditional places of worship such as churches or temples. Some read holy books, such as the Bible or the Quran. Some pray, some meditate, some practise Buddhism (which, as far as I understand it, is not a religion), and some do yoga. There are many other activities that are aimed a nurturing the spiritual being. Whatever it is that you do to sharpen the soul, you do it in your capacity as a spiritual being – separate and distinct from all the other shades of yourself. And it should be recognised as precisely that.

The soul is what guides the conscience, and it is what gives rise to guilt and many other emotions. These are feelings that machines, despite their high levels of intelligence, will never have.

- *You, just you*

Finally, just you!

This effectively captures everything that doesn't fall into any of the other shades of life. It includes all of the things that you like to do purely because they give you personal pleasure. This could be watching TV, playing golf, reading, hiking, or whatever you just like to do. It's necessary for all of us to spend time doing these things. Be careful not to let this fade into oblivion as you develop more shades of yourself – commonly *you, the spouse*, and *you, the parent* – and there seems to be less and less time to allocate to the increasing number of shades.

At first glance, it's easy to place two or three life shades into one box, and count that box as one. For example, as we saw above, once you've had children, you might conflate the life shade *you, the spouse* with that of *you, the parent*. Using the analogy of different shades of colour to explain the different aspects of life is apt since, just as different shades of colour blend into one another, so too does it appear as if different aspects of life blend so that they become one and the same. However, this is a mistake. This is where people go wrong. It means one or more shades are being totally neglected. With neglect comes regret.

Let me give an analogy to better illustrate this. One that every parent can certainly identify with and that, I'm pretty sure, even non-parents can easily understand. Let's say that, like I do, you have two children who are fairly close to each other in age. In your eyes as a parent, your two children are nearly identical. You feed them the same food, you send them to the same school, you bath them together (up to a certain age), and you love them to the same degree (albeit in slightly different ways). But despite all this, you are always very well aware of the fact that they are two separate and distinct individuals. Each of them must be, and is, recognised and treated as an individual in her or his own right. If you were simply to annex Child A to Child B, and to treat them as one, the whole persona and being of Child A will effectively be neglected and abandoned.

The same applies to every shade of you!

APPENDIX B

HOW THE LAW TURNED DEBTORS INTO KINGS

Zimbabwe has just entered hyperinflation territory or, at the best, is on the verge of doing so. Zimbabwe has just seen a host of monetary reforms being implemented, including an overnight currency change. Zimbabwe, as an inevitable result, has seen rippling effects across the economic landscape. So, what does all this mean to the legal landscape?

As a practising attorney soon after the turn of the century, I always found it an unenviable task to explain to a client how the legal process to recover money owed to them would take 18-24 months. This was, and remains, a function of the well-defined *dies induciae* for each stage of the litigation process as rightfully prescribed in the Rules of Court, coupled with the relative ease with which unscrupulous litigants and lawyers alike can and do manipulate the legal process. Having left private practice and moved into the business sector as In-House Counsel some ten years ago, I continue to find it equally difficult to convey this same message to internal clients.

Now, to add to the already unsavoury state of

affairs any creditor already found themselves in because the inflationary environment combined with the largely unavoidable drawn-out nature of the legal process and its equally unavoidable abuse, 2019 saw the arrival of a new and far more dangerous beast for creditors and their lawyers to contend with – Statutory Instrument 33 of 2019 ("SI 33"). For purposes of this article, I shall not delve into the validity of this Statutory Instrument when looked at in light of the Constitution of Zimbabwe and established principles of law including the fact that it is a piece of subsidiary legislation purporting to amend existing Acts of Parliament.

SI 33 was gazetted on 22 February 2019. One of its major impacts was to officially confirm the long-standing *de facto* distinction between the United States Dollar ("USD") and the RTGS or Bond Dollar (hereinafter referred to simply as "RTGS"), and the concurrent creation of an official exchange rate. Its more devastating effect, however, was to convert any amount owed in USD to RTGS at a rate of 1:1 despite the disparity prevailing in reality. The relevant wording is:

> "all assets and liabilities that were, immediately before the effective date, valued and expressed in United States dollars (other than assets and liabilities referred to in section 44C(2) of the principal Act) shall on and after the effective date be deemed to be values in RTGS dollars at a rate of one-to-one to the United States dollar"

Appendix B

The exceptions are irrelevant and immaterial to the content of this article.

So where did this leave a creditor? The denomination of debt in USD, which was essentially the one and only measure available to creditors to mitigate against this inherent time-factor risk arising from the lengthy legal process, was suddenly rendered unenforceable at law.

The reality of the situation needs to be explained and contextualized, particularly for those who are not in Zimbabwe.

Prior to the gazetting of SI 33, Zimbabwe had no official currency of its own, and traded primarily in USD. At some point around 2016, a quasi-currency called the Bond note was introduced, later becoming known, interchangeably, as the RTGS dollar. The USD and RTGS were officially said to be at par. i.e. USD1 = RTGS1. It was literally impossible, however, to physically exchange that RTGS1 for USD1 through any official (or unofficial) channel. This meant, unsurprisingly, that there was a very lucrative black-market for currency exchange. The black-market rate at the time of the gazetting of SI 33 was approximately 4. i.e. USD1 = RTGS4.

As mentioned, SI 33 did away with this theoretical and farcical parity between the USD and RTGS. The starting official rate was 2.5. i.e. USD1 = RTGS2.50. But, again, it was all but impossible to exchange currency at this official rate of 2.5 through official channels. The black-market continued to thrive.

In less than 4 months, the official exchange rate had climbed to approximately 6.5. i.e. USD1 = RTGS6-50. But so had the black-market rate, which was up to approximately 12. i.e. USD1 = RTGS12.

So, in reality, what does all this mean to a debtor who, for argument sake, owed USD120 on 21 February 2019?

- On 21 February 2019, the debt was legally denominated in USD, in the amount of USD120.
- On 22 February, literally overnight, the debt suddenly became RTGS120. This had an (unrealistic) official value USD48. The realistic value of that RTGS120, using the black-market rate, was USD30.
- Within 4 months, this RTGS120 had an (unrealistic) official value of USD18-50, and a realistic value of USD10 using the black-market rate.

With this background and context, it becomes easy to see that the law reduced all debt by 75% overnight, and by 92% in 4 months.

Unsurprisingly, there have been attempts by some to tame this beast that is SI 33 through the courts, but these remain matters *sub judice*. The High Court of Zimbabwe (HH 428-19; HC4747/19) passed judgment in June 2019 to the effect

Appendix B

that, notwithstanding the wording of SI 33, the conversion of debt from USD to RTGS at 1:1 does **not** apply to judgment debts in place at the time of gazetting. Unsurprisingly, this has been referred by the debtor, to the Supreme Court of Zimbabwe on appeal.

It is an age-old adage that the law is an ass. But we now come to see that over and above being an ass, the law can turn debtors into kings!

Notes

1. https://news.gallup.com/opinion/chairman/212045/world-broken-workplace.aspx?g_source=position1&g_medium=related&g_campaign=tiles.
2. https://en.wikipedia.org/wiki/The_World%27s_Billionaires - The World's Billionaires - Wikipedia
3. Pillay, M. (2019), *Life Demystified: Understanding – The Secret to Success*, Second Edition pp94-98.
4. Duhigg, C. (2013) *The Power of Habit. Why we do what we do and how to change*, p 77.
5. Duhigg, C. (2013) *The Power of Habit*, p 270.
6. https://www.psychologytoday.com/us/blog/deconstructing-illness/202112/happiness-vs-pleasure-the-source-our-discontent
7. Duhigg, C. (2013) *The Power of Habit*, pp 245-246
8. Mander, A.E. *Psychology for Everyman* (1935) pp 18-19
9. Hill, N. *Think and Grow Rich: The Secret to Freedom and Success* (2021) p141.
10. Pillay, M. (2020) *The Different Shades of You: Your Guide to Genuine Fulfilment* pp 21-29
11. Pillay, M. (2020) *The Different Shades of You* pp33-35
12. Pillay, M. (2020) *The Different Shades of You* p 48
13. Jepson, R. W. *Clear Thinking* Fourth Edition (1948) p 111
14. Jepson, R. W. *Clear Thinking* pp 114-115
15. https://money.cnn.com/2011/12/21/markets/world_markets_ecb/index.htm - World markets spike then pull back on news of ECB injection - Dec. 21, 2011 (cnn.com)
16. https://www.theguardian.com/world/2008/oct/09/Zimbabwe - Zimbabwe's inflation rate surges to 231,000,000% | Zimbabwe | The Guardian

17. https://www.bbc.com/news/world-middle-east-62514631 - Lebanon man hailed hero for holding Beirut bank hostage over savings - BBC News
18. https://markets.businessinsider.com/news/currencies/80-trillion-off-balance-sheet-debt-blind-spot-financial-system-2022-12
19. https://www.visualcapitalist.com/visualizing-65-trillion-in-hidden-dollar-debt/
20. https://www.express.co.uk/finance/personalfinance/1706328/Financial-crisis-FX-swap-market-central-bankers-80-trillion-crash-meltdown-BIS
21. https://moneywise.com/investing/stocks/the-stocks-had-the-worst-days-ever
22. https://www.bloomberg.com/news/articles/2022-12-30/elon-musk-becomes-first-person-ever-to-lose-200-billion
23. https://en.wikipedia.org/wiki/Bernie_Madoff - Bernie Madoff - Wikipedia
24. Gladwell, M. (2019) *Talking to Strangers: What we should know about the people we don't know.* pp89-90
25. Pillay, M. *The Different Shades of You* Pp37-37
26. https://www.bls.gov/news.release/empsit.t19.htm - Table B-3. Average hourly and weekly earnings of all employees on private nonfarm payrolls by industry sector, seasonally adjusted - 2023 M03 Results (bls.gov)
27. https://www.fidelity.com/insights/investing-ideas/best-return-investment - Average return on investment: What is a good return? (fidelity.com)
28. https://www.forbes.com/sites/jacobwolinsky/2022/08/30/heres-how-the-

top-50-hedge-funds-generate-consistent-returns/?sh=50de99dd3faf - Here's How The "Top 50" Hedge Funds Generate Consistent Returns (forbes.com)
29. Kahneman, D (2012) *Thinking, Fast and Slow* pp 396-397
30. Pillay, M (2020) *Corporate Culture Demystified: Why Good Business Strategies Fail* p 115
31. https://www.cnbc.com/2019/02/13/billionaire-warren-buffett-says-this-is-the-only-measure-of-success-that-matters.html - Warren Buffett: This is the greatest measure of success in life (cnbc.com)
32. Gladwell, M – *Outliers* pp 5-11
33. Pillay, M *Life Demystified* (Second Ed) pp28-29
34. Duhigg, C. (2013) *The Power of Habit*, p270
35. Butler-Bowdon, T. *50 Success Classics: Winning Wisdom for Work & Life from 50 Landmark Books* (2004) p.204
36. Gladwell, M (2009) *Outliers – The Story of Success* p268
37. https://en.wikipedia.org/wiki/Tiger_Woods - Tiger Woods - Wikipedia
38. https://en.wikipedia.org/wiki/Diego_Maradona - Diego Maradona - Wikipedia
39. Duhigg, C. (2013) *The Power of Habit*, p110
40. https://en.wikipedia.org/wiki/Michael_Phelps - Michael Phelps - Wikipedia
41. Gladwell, M. *Outliers* pp22-23
42. Gladwell, M. *Outliers* pp50-55
43. Gladwell M. *Outliers* p39

www.ingramcontent.com/pod-product-compliance
Lightning Source LLC
Chambersburg PA
CBHW060554080526
44585CB00013B/566